Dr. Raul Valverde

Principles of Human Computer Interaction Design

Dr. Raul Valverde

Principles of Human Computer Interaction Design

HCI Design

LAP LAMBERT Academic Publishing

Impressum/Imprint (nur für Deutschland/only for Germany)
Bibliografische Information der Deutschen Nationalbibliothek: Die Deutsche
Nationalbibliothek verzeichnet diese Publikation in der Deutschen Nationalbibliografie;
detaillierte bibliografische Daten sind im Internet über http://dnb.d-nb.de abrufbar.
Alle in diesem Buch genannten Marken und Produktnamen unterliegen warenzeichen-,
marken- oder patentrechtlichem Schutz bzw. sind Warenzeichen oder eingetragene
Warenzeichen der jeweiligen Inhaber. Die Wiedergabe von Marken, Produktnamen,
Gebrauchsnamen, Handelsnamen, Warenbezeichnungen u.s.w. in diesem Werk berechtigt
auch ohne besondere Kennzeichnung nicht zu der Annahme, dass solche Namen im Sinne
der Warenzeichen- und Markenschutzgesetzgebung als frei zu betrachten wären und
daher von jedermann benutzt werden dürften.

Coverbild: www.ingimage.com

Verlag: LAP LAMBERT Academic Publishing GmbH & Co. KG
Dudweiler Landstr. 99, 66123 Saarbrücken, Deutschland
Telefon +49 681 3720-310, Telefax +49 681 3720-3109
Email: info@lap-publishing.com

Herstellung in Deutschland:
Schaltungsdienst Lange o.H.G., Berlin
Books on Demand GmbH, Norderstedt
Reha GmbH, Saarbrücken
Amazon Distribution GmbH, Leipzig
ISBN: 978-3-8454-1462-1

Imprint (only for USA, GB)
Bibliographic information published by the Deutsche Nationalbibliothek: The Deutsche
Nationalbibliothek lists this publication in the Deutsche Nationalbibliografie; detailed
bibliographic data are available in the Internet at http://dnb.d-nb.de.
Any brand names and product names mentioned in this book are subject to trademark,
brand or patent protection and are trademarks or registered trademarks of their respective
holders. The use of brand names, product names, common names, trade names, product
descriptions etc. even without a particular marking in this works is in no way to be
construed to mean that such names may be regarded as unrestricted in respect of
trademark and brand protection legislation and could thus be used by anyone.

Cover image: www.ingimage.com

Publisher: LAP LAMBERT Academic Publishing GmbH & Co. KG
Dudweiler Landstr. 99, 66123 Saarbrücken, Germany
Phone +49 681 3720-310, Fax +49 681 3720-3109
Email: info@lap-publishing.com

Printed in the U.S.A.
Printed in the U.K. by (see last page)
ISBN: 978-3-8454-1462-1

Principles of Human Computer Interaction Design

Table of Contents

Preface

This book covers the design, evaluation and development process for interactive human computer interfaces. User interface design principles, task analysis, interface design methods, auditory interfaces, haptics, user interface evaluation and usability testing are introduced with the use of examples. The goal of this book is to raise awareness for the importance of user-centered principles to the design of good interfaces. Human aspects are covered and analyzed as the base for the design of user interfaces and their implementation.

Topics covered include: human capabilities and limitations, the interface design and engineering process, prototyping, issues in interface construction, interface evaluation, and World Wide Web and mobile device interface issues.

The book is ideal for the student that wants to learn how to use prototyping tools as part of the interface design and how to evaluate an interface and its interaction quality by using usability testing techniques.

Chapter 1

Interaction paradigms

Welcome to Human Computer Interaction! The next eight chapters are about the theory, design, evaluation and development process for interactive application interfaces. However, what exactly is Human Computer Interaction?

Human Computer Interaction

According to Baecker, Grudin, Buxton, and Greenberg (1995). HCI is the "discipline concerned with the design, evaluation, and implementation of interacting computing systems". Humans interact with a computing system via a human-computer interface. A human-computer interface focuses in three main components (Rees et al. 2001):

1. The human
2. The computing system (machine)
3. The interaction

HCI is critical in the development of software and hardware systems; you might have a powerful software application with many features but if the user is not able to operate it easily, he or she will discard it after few trials. In order to improve the usability of a software package, HCI specialists endeavor to:

- Understand psychological, organizational, and social factors of the combined human and computer system.
- Develop methodologies to aid appropriate HCI design.
- Realize efficient and effective interactions for single users and groups.

All of these efforts are directed at putting the user's requirements ahead of the technology as stated above. The system should be tailored for people, not the other way round.

Computing Environments

Since HCI specialists need to understand psychological, organizational, and social factors of the combined human and computer system in order build competitive interfaces for software and hardware systems, it is important to explore the social, physical and cognitive environments and evaluate their effect in building interfaces.

Physical Computing Environment affects many aspects of an interface 's design. For this, the designer of an interface needs to take into consideration the ergonomics of the system. Ergonomics can be defined as "fitting the system to the human" (Robin Good, 2004). One of the goals of ergonomics is to create a safe computing environment by designing a system that protects the welfare of the user, issues as device radiation should be a concern for the interface designer.

Physical Computing Environment is also concerned about the working and user space, the user must be able to have enough room to use the interface without difficulties and enough working space to bring the work objects such as notebooks and PDAs required to accomplish his or her work. In addition, interface designers must ensure enough lighting, efficiency, low levels of noise and pollution as part of their design.

The social environment affects the way people use computers. Different computing paradigms imply different social environments. For instance, personal computing is usually a solitary activity done in an office or an isolated corner of the house. Mobile computing is often done outside and in public places. Social environment should be taken into consideration when designing interfaces. For example, Machines like ATMs, that are in most cases located in public areas, must preserve the user's privacy.

Cognitive Computing Environment looks at the cognitive aspects involved with the interaction between people and computers. These are issues which originate in the cognitive sciences and include basic psychological concepts such as learning and problem solving in terms of abilities, strategies, knowledge and styles.

When designing an interface, the designer should take into consideration cognitive issues such as age, disabilities, degree of focus and degree of technical knowledge of users. In addition, computers are used in diverse environments that impose different levels of cognitive stress on the user, this means that the interface needs to be aware if an interface is for a mission-critical application that requires a clear and unambiguous interface that leaves no room for error or if the interface is for leisure activities such as listening to music that might require a more pleasant interface rather than a complex interface that is designed for a high level cognitive stress.

5W + H

The "who, what, where, why, and how" (5W+H) heuristic is a procedure that can be used to define and analyze existing interaction paradigms and spaces and explore the elements and objects with which the user interacts (Heim, 2007).

The heuristic has three components:

- The What/How : This is used to understand the physical and virtual interface components. For example, I/O devices, windows, icons, etc.
- Where/When: This is related to physical environment. It looks at the differences between office, portable, wearable systems.
- Who/Why: This looks at the types of tasks and skill sets required.

Interaction paradigms

An interaction paradigm is a model or pattern of human–computer interaction that encompasses all aspects of interaction, including physical, virtual, perceptual, and cognitive (Heim 2007).

The interaction paradigms identified by Heim (2007) and shown in figure 1.3 in the textbook are:
- Large Scale Computing
- Personal Computing
- Networked Computing
- Mobile Computing
- Collaborative Environments
- Virtual Reality
- Augmented Reality

The 5W+H heuristic is used to describe the paradigms indicated below:

Large scale computing paradigm

What/How- The large scale computing paradigm includes mainframe computers that were large computers and they resided in a central location. These computers were accessed by remote alphanumeric terminals ("dumb terminals") equipped with keyboards. These started as electronic typewriter and later developed to CRT screens. Large-scale computing includes super computers which are specialized machines that crunch large amounts of data at high speed, as in computing fluid dynamics, weather patterns, seismic activity predictions, and nuclear explosion dynamics. Display, other then text, was produced on special and expensive devices such as plotters or customized CRTs.

When/Where- Most large computers were owned by government agencies and large research institutes affiliated with large universities.

Who/Why- Large-scale computing resources are expensive and generally used to carry out government sponsored-research projects and university-based research for large corporate institutions. Supercomputers are used for the very high speed backbone (vBNS) connections that constitute the core of the Internet while mainframes are still in use in the financial industry.

Personal computing paradigm

The personal computing paradigm is driven by Graphical User Interfaces (GUI) and found in commercial operating systems such as Windows and Macintosh. The Alto computer developed at the Xerox Palo Alto Research Center in 1973, was the first computer to use a GUI that involved the desktop metaphor: pop-up menus, windows, and icons. This was later adopted by Apple for their Lisa and Macs machines, and later on by the Windows operating system of Microsoft. The development started the personal computer paradigm that includes Desktop and Personal-Public Computing. This paradigm is analyzed by using the 5W+H heuristic in the following two sections.

Personal computing paradigm (Desktop)

What/How- This model can be defied as a single computer with a keyboard and pointing device interacting with software applications and Internet resources. A desktop can have permanent media storage like CDs and DVD ROMS and portable hard drive technologies such as large capacity arrays and pen-sized USB sticks.

Where/When- Desktop PCs are available for home and office use and entertainment.

Who/Why- PCs are used for many applications. Productivity tools as word processing, spreadsheet and presentation software are used in the office environment. Computer games and E-commerce applications as banking are used by home users. Modern PCs are as powerful as where the Large Scale computer of previous generations.

Public-Personal computing paradigm

Public access computers are part of this paradigm. Public access computers include ATM machines, Mall directories, electronic boards and electronic advertisements.

What/How- Public access computers are normally implemented with regular PC desktop computers with security that prevent access to operating systems functions and protects the computer against viruses or other potential security threats. They most often take the form of information kiosks or ticket-dispensing machines and their interfaces use touch screen devices.

Where/When- Public access computers are found in many indoor and outdoor installations like government offices, banks, malls and theaters.

Who/Why- This type of computers are used by the general public and normally used to access public information, access public services and conduct financial transactions for banking and payment for services.

Networking computing paradigm

What/How- A network is a communications, data exchange, and resource-sharing system created by linking two or more computers and establishing standards, or protocols, so that they can work together. Networks can be classified based on their scope: Wide Area Network (WAN), Metropolitan Area Network (MAN), Local Area Network (LAN) and Personal Area Network (PAN). Networks can also be classified based on their transmission media: Wired Media and Wireless Media. This paradigm is enabled by several technologies Ethernet and TCP/IP protocols, personal computer and telephone networks and modems

Where/When- Computer networks have freed users from location-based computing since users can access internet based systems like e-mail and web browsers from any location that has internet access. Network resources can be accessed at any time without restriction.

Who/Why- People from all backgrounds and ages are using the internet on an every day basis. From banking to online games, users worldwide access network based applications for a wide range of interests.

Mobile computing paradigm

What/How- Mobile computing paradigm includes technologies that comprise a very diverse family of devices. This paradigm includes the devices mentioned below:
- Laptop computers
- Tablet computers
- Game players
- MP3 players
- MP4 Players
- PDAs
- Wearable computers
- Cell phones

Mobile devices can be connected to global positioning systems (GPS). These have touch screens and voice interaction to alleviate potential visual attention problems during driving.

Where/When- Mobiles devices liberate users from the need to be at a specific location. Wi-Fi internet access is nowadays available at most of the public places including airports, coffee shops, hotels and malls. Wearable computers can be worn by users at any time and any place and ideal for health monitoring application. Mobile devices can offer situational computing that can take advantage of location-specific information through location-based mobile services (LMS). LMS can be beneficial for location-sensitive advertisements, public service announcements, social interactions, and location-specific educational information.

Who/Why- Business users benefit greatly from mobile computing. The ability to have access to e-mail and remote databases when being away from the office, is of great benefit to business in general. However, mobile computing has potential for most of the aspects of the human life as e-commerce, health care, entertainment among others.

Collaborative environment paradigm

What/How - In a collaborative environment paradigm, computer networks allow members of a group to interact with other members on shared files and documents. This creates a virtual space where people can collaborate and work collectively with the use of Computer-mediated communication (CMC).

A groupware is a CMC that allows remote interaction by using synchronous technologies such as video conferencing, instant messaging and chat rooms or asynchronous technologies such as e-mail, bulleting boards and discussion groups.

An example of a collaborative environment is the *collaboratory*. Wulf (1989) called the collaboratory "a center without walls, in which the nation's researchers can perform their research without regard to physical location-interacting with colleagues, accessing instrumentation, sharing data and computational resources, and accessing information in digital libraries.".

Where/When- *Computer supported cooperative work* (CSCW) (Galegher, Kraut, & Egido, 1990) is computer-assisted coordinated activity such as problem solving and communication carried out by a group of collaborating individuals. The multi-user software supporting CSCW systems is known as *groupware*. A groupware can be based on remote interaction using synchronous technologies like video conferencing or asynchronous technologies like email and discussion groups.

Who/Why- CMC is used in business in order to eliminate transportation costs since it helps to collaborate with remote customers or employees. Engineering benefits as well from this paradigm as it facilitates the collaboration of engineering teams spread at different locations. Universities use CMC to facilitate e-learning and research, an example of this is the Research Collaboratory for Structural Bioinformatics (RCSB, 2005).

An obvious example to the collaborative paradigm is our online MSc in computing programs that you are using, as well as other online education projects.

Virtual reality paradigm
What/How -The virtual reality paradigm offer users a computer simulated alternative to the real world. Virtual reality technologies can be divided into two distinct groups:
• Nonimmersive environments
• Immersive environments

Non-immersive environments are screen-based, pointer-driven, three-dimensional (3D) graphical presentations that may involve haptic technology feedback as Virtual Reality Virtual Modeling language and QuickTime VR. Haptic technology refers to technology which interfaces the user via the sense of touch by applying forces, vibrations and/or motions to the

5

user. Successful systems that provide 3D virtual world experience are the Second Life and the Active Worlds Internet offrings.

Immersive VR environments are designed to create a sense of "being" in a world populated by virtual objects. To create a convincing illusion, they must use as many human perceptual channels as possible. Virtual Reality immersive I/O devices include:

- Head Mounted Display (HMD) (http://www.sensics.com/)
- Spatial Immersive Display (SID)
- Cave Automated Virtual Environment (CAVE) (http://brighton.ncsa.uiuc.edu/~prajlich/cave.html)
- Head-movement-tracking systems
- Passive systems
- Active locomotion systems

When/Where-VR systems are found in large scientific research laboratories in the government and in engineering firms.

Who/Why- VR offers benefits in fields like aerospace, medical, military and in general domains that require expensive environments for training. One example of a company that develops VR systems for flight simulators in the military is CAE electronics in Montreal Canada (http://www.cae.com). In Psychology it has application for the treatment of phobias. VR is also used to implement Computer-aided design software used in systems as Cadence used for IC design (http://www.cadence.com/).

Augmented Reality paradigm

What/How- The goal of Augmented Reality (AR) is to create a seamless integration between real and virtual objects in a way that augments the user's perception and experience. Azuma (1997) defines an augmented reality system as one that

- combines real and virtual
- is interactive in real time
- is registered in 3D

Criteria for AR environments are that the virtual information must be relevant to and in synchronization with the real-world environment.

AR I/O devices include:

- Heads Up Displays (HUD) (E.g. Critical data viewer http://microoptical.net/)
- Motorcycle helmets (E.g. Sportvue http://www.sportvue.com/)

Where/When- AR technology is applicable in situations in which people need access to computing functionality and cannot afford to leave their work site. Emergency professionals as firemen and police could benefit from such systems since they could access information as building blueprints that could help in an emergency situation.

Who/Why- Current applications include military and emergency applications services (e.g. showing maps, instructions, enemy locations, fire cells), simulation (e.g. flight and driving simulators), navigation devices (e.g. cars and airplanes), games (e.g. ARQuake) and education among others.

6

Summary

HCI is the discipline concerned with the design, evaluation, and implementation of interacting computing systems. HCI specialists need to understand the social, physical and cognitive environments and their effects as part of the interface design process. The Large Scale Computing, Personal Computing, Networked Computing, Mobile Computing, Collaborative Environments, Virtual Reality and Augmented Reality paradigms were analyzed with the 5W+H heuristic process.

References

Azuma, R. T. 1997, 'A Survey of Augmented Reality.' *Presence: Teleoperators and Virtual Environments*, vol. 6, no. 4, pp. 355 – 385.

Baecker, R. 1991, 'New paradigms for computing in the nineties', *Proceedings Graphics Interface*, pp. 224-229

Baecker, R., Grudin, J., Buxton, W., & Greenberg, S. 1995, *Readings in Human Computer Interaction: Towards the Year 2000 (2nd Edition)*, Morgan-Kaufmann. US

Galegher, J., Kraut, R., & Egido, C. 1990, *Intellectual Teamwork: Social and Technological Foundations of Cooperative Work*, Lawrence Erlbaum Associates.

Heim, S. 2007, The Resonant Interface HCI Foundations for interaction design, Addison Wesley.

Cogburn, D. L. 2003, 'HCI in the so-called developing world: what's in it for everyone', *Interactions,* vol.10, no.2, pp. 80-87.

RCSB, 2005, Welcome to the RCSB PDB. Retrieved December 23, 2006 from [Online] Available http://www.rcsb.org/ [Accessed 8 Nov 2007]

Rees M., White A. & Bebo W. 2001, *Designing Web Interfaces*, Prentice Hall

Discussion questions

1. Research an existing interaction paradigm and write a report on some of the hardware used. Discuss how it works, and then follow the 5W+H heuristic to explain how and why it is appropriate for the paradigm.

2. Pick a particular type of computer peripheral, such as an input or output device. Trace the evolution in this device in terms of changes in both user interface characteristics and breadth of choices.

3. Discuss the commercial and social potential benefits of such systems as Second Life and Active Worlds. Do you regard them as a passing interest, or do you believe they are here to stay? Would there mark be felt in the future?

4. Discuss the observed why so many Human Computer Interactions disappeared from the market, leaving the field mostly to the WEB/HTML/CSS. Have we gained or lost about this convergence?

5. Discuss the Human computer Interaction of the online system that we use in our programme (FirstClass). Highlights both its pros and cons of tits HCI.

Activities

Complete the following set of tasks

Design a situational computing environment using existing hardware and software technologies. Explain how it will work and define the following:

  a. 5W + H Heuristic
  b. Computing Paradigm
  c. Physical Computing Environment
  d. Social Computing Environment
  e. Cognitive Computing Environment

Sample Answer for Activity

We will analyze the internet café (wiki, 2010) as the computing environment.
There are already suitable hardware and software technologies to enable this environment to be created.
- Standard desktop computer with monitor
- Internet connection
- Web browser software
- Suitable accommodation, premises
- Furniture etc

How will it work?
Users wishing to check there email or browse the internet may not have easy access to a computer of their own. So for a small fee they can enter the shop and purchase online time from the owner. Since this is going to be a public service it needs to be located in a central place, like a high street in town, and the opening times need to be varied. Many people may not be able to get to the shop during office hours so a late night close would be necessary. The shop could also offer printing facilities at a charge per print. Many games are now multiplayer utilising the internet as a means of connecting people wishing to play these co-op games. They are also more widely known as mmoprg (wiki, 2010). This is another facility the shop may wish to provide.
Let's analyze the proposal using 5W+H heuristic approach
What/How
This service will provide the general public with internet access which will enable them to
- Access email
- Browse the internet
- Play co-op Games

It will also provide them with a suitable environment into which to engage in this activity. A charge will be levied for each hour the member of the public is using this service.
Where/When

In order to make the café accessible it's important that the location is central to as many people as possible, a town high street for instance. The opening times are very important. During office hours the café may not be very busy but during rush hour when people are travelling home from work they are most likely wants to pop in to check email. The times the café is open may need to be varied and this can finally tune as time goes on. In order to work with members of the public the following open times may be used.

Open	Close	
10:00	13:30	Catches the lunch time crowd
16:30	22:00	Caters for rush hour commuters etc.

Who/why
Personnel computers can be expensive and in today's modern world each home is slowly becoming digitally connected, but we are not all there yet. Just like VCR's in the 1970's it will take time for the public to catch up. The café fills this interim gap by allowing people who may not have the funds for their own computer to engage with the modern world so to speak. It may also help those who are a little nervous of this technology to try it out before they invest their own money for a unit of their own.
This café would come under the public-personnel computing paradigm as the café offers public access to various types of information.
The physical computing environment or the ergonomics of it must provide a safe environment in which the café operates. This must include the café

- Suitable desk with enough room
- Sufficient lighting
- Suitable seating
- Arm and wrist rests
- Adjustable monitor stands to prevent neck strain
- Screen filters where needed to prevent eye strain
- Foot Rests
- No trailing cables which could represent a trip hazard
- Ergonomic (Ergonomics, 2010) Keyboards and mice
- Access and facilities for the disabled. (ucandoit, 2010)

The social environment may also need to be considered. Although this is a public access service individuals may still want privacy. Therefore screens maybe employed to isolate individuals in there own working environment. Special filters on monitors can be used which prevent people viewing private information from an angle. Where audio is used for video conferencing, rather than use speakers, headphones should be used for added privacy.
Using the cognitive approach which manly deals with how people interact with computers, we must ensure that the system employed overall is easy to use and requires little or now introduction for the user. The interface, or browser, must be initiative enough for the user to get up and running virtually straight away. As many aspects of the system should be automated as possible to ensure the user has a pleasant experience. For instance as regards to security things like anti-virus protection should be in place to protect the user and be totally transparent to the user, as should things like firewalls.
A familiar style of computing should be used to which the majority of the public is used too. So no fancy shop designed interface that needs navigating before you can access the internet.

References
En.wikipedia.org Internet Café [online] Available from
http://en.wikipedia.org/wiki/Internet_caf%C3%A9 (Accessed 12th October 2010)
www.en.wikipedia.org MMORPG [online] Available from
http://en.wikipedia.org/wiki/Massively_multiplayer_online_role-playing_game (Accessed 12th October 2010)

www.ergonomics.org.uk Ergonomics [online] Available from http://www.ergonomics.org.uk/ (Accessed 12th October 2010)
www.ucandoit.org.uk Home Page [online] Available from http://www.ucandoit.org.uk/ucandoit/index.php (Accessed 12th October 2010)

Chapter 2

Interaction frameworks and styles

In this chapter, the concept of interaction framework will be examined together with the different interaction styles used in interface design. Command line, menu based, forms, question answer, Web, 3D, natural language interaction styles will be covered in detail.

Interaction framework

Human interaction with machinery is complex and cannot be quantified easily. One way to put structure into this process is with the use of interaction frameworks. A framework is a structure that provides a context for conceptualizing something. Frameworks present a global view of an interaction (Dix et al 1998). In addition, frameworks help to identify problematic areas within the design.

Execution/Evaluation Action Cycle

The Execution/Evaluation Action Cycle is an HCI model proposed by Norman (1990) which explores the nature of actions and how they are structured. The structure of an action has four basic parts: 1) The goal – what is to be achieved; 2) Execution – the actual action execution; 3) World – the manipulation of items in the world via the execution of the action; and 4) Evaluation – the analysis of the changes to the world compared to the intended goal.

The goal does not necessarily define a single action, rather the goal is represented as intentions that identify the specific actions required to achieve the goal. The key is to remember that many sequences of actions may lead to accomplishing a goal. Donald Norman's (1998) Interaction framework consists in seven action stages: 1) Establishing the goal; 2) Forming an intention; 3) Specifying the action sequence; and 4) Executing the action sequence. Once an action has been completed, humans assess the outcome of the action during the evaluation phase. This particular phase has three additional stages: 1) perceiving the current world state; 2) Interpreting the percepts; and 3) Evaluating the percept interpretation and comparing the results to the goal. These three steps combined with the four action steps provide seven steps (or stages) of action.

Understanding how humans define their goals, establish intentions, carry out actions, and assess the action outcomes is an important step when developing an interface. As the systems become more complex, understanding the elements of the Execution/Evaluation Action cycle become more difficult because they incorporate more complex cognitive factors. These factors are the focus of this lecture.

Norman's model concentrates on user's view of the interface. It assumes that some systems are harder to use than others. The model defines *gulfs that* represent the difficulties that user might have in accomplishing an interface task from the execution and evaluation points of view. Norman defined the terms Gulf of Execution and Gulf of Evaluation. The Gulf of Execution refers to the situation in which the human formulates an intention to carry out an action but the system does not provide the capability to complete the action. The Gulf of Evaluation occurs when the human is able to execute the desired action, but is unable to evaluate the outcome of the action. The Gulf of Evaluation occurs when the system does not provide sufficient feedback to the human.

A gulf of execution measures how different is the user's formulation of actions from the actions allowed by the system. Let's assume that a user has the goal to save a file, given this goal the user has the intention to use the file system and this leads him or her to perform the action of selecting the save option of the interface. Since the action requires the interface to support a save option, the system could have a gulf of execution if the interface does not present a save option.

A gulf of evaluation measures how different is the user's expectation of changed system state from the actual presentation of this state. For example, if the file system in the previous example is not clearly visible and located where the user would expect it to be located, this could create a gulf of evaluation.

Some questions that might be helpful to determine if an interface presents a gulf of evaluation are identified by Norman (1990) below:

- How easily can the user determine what the device's function is?
- How easily can the user determine what actions are possible with the device?
- How easily can the user determine how intentions are mapped to physical movement?
- How easily can the user determine if an action has been performed?
- How easily can the user determine if the system is in the desired state?
- How easily can the user determine the mapping from the system state to interpretation?
- How easily can the user determine the state the system is actually in?

Dix et. al Interaction framework

Dix et. al (1998) expanded on the EEC model to include the system. Their interaction framework has 4 parts as indicated in figure 1.

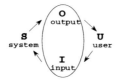

Figure 1 Interaction Framework

This is a general framework for understanding interaction that is not restricted to electronic computer systems. It identifies all major components involved in interaction and allows comparative assessment of systems.

The framework assumes that both user and system have their own unique language and the interaction facilitates translation between languages. Any problem with the interaction is due to problems in the translation between user and system languages.

The framework shows how user intentions are translated into actions at the interface level. These actions are then translated into alterations of the system state. Alterations of the system state are reflected in the output display that it is then interpreted by the user.

Coping with Complexity

Interaction design is a complex task due to the level of abstraction required to understand the user's viewpoint. Different tools can be used to cope with this complexity, including mental models, mapping, semantic and articulatory distance and affordances (Heim 2007).

Norman (1983) introduced the concept of user's mental model of a computer system with which the user is interacting. This computer system should communicate the *conceptual model*, which is an accurate, consistent, and complete representation of the target system held by the designer, or an expert user, of the system. The user's mental model is formulated through interaction with the computer system, and constantly modified throughout the interaction. This model is a cognitive representation of something that defines a logical and believable estimation as to how an object is constructed or how it functions. Metal models can help to model the user's view. This model can be used to align the interaction's design with the user's view in order to facilitate its use.

Young (1983) introduced task-action mapping models. Young linked the internalised representation of the system to the real-world task which users have to perform. Task-action mappings describe the structure of a real-world task and the actions needed to perform that task, and provide a direct mapping between the task and the corresponding actions. Young (1981) uses the example of an algebraic calculator for a mapping model: the operations that have to be performed can be mapped onto doing the same task with paper and pencil. A task-action mapping model would allow competent use of a system for a particular task, even though the user has no detailed knowledge of the system and how it works.

Another two important tools used in interaction design are: semantic and articulary distances. Semantic distance is a tool that measures the distance between what people want to do and the meaning of an interface element, while the articulatory distance measures the distance between the physical appearance of an interface element and what it actually means (Heim 2007).

Affordances are tools that represent connections that allow us to make predictions about the results of our actions and help us to create usable mental models. These connections are user's interpretations of the interface, these can be obvious such a turning wheel that affords turning but sometime confusing. This interface shows text boxes used as labels for a log in interface that allow input when the purpose to provide an output.

Interaction Styles

The way users interact with computers is referred to as interaction style (Heim 2007). A list of interaction styles is given below:

- Command Line
- Menu-Based Interface
- Form Fill-In

- Spreadsheets
- Question and Answer
- Direct Manipulation
- Metaphors
- Web Navigation
- Three-Dimensional Environments
- Zoomable Interface
- Natural Language

Command Line

Command-line style is used by Operating Systems such as Linux, Unix and MS-DOS and it is mainly based on text commands. It has the advantage of being very fast compared to other more graphical interfaces. In addition, Command-Line interfaces tend to be very flexible since commands can be created with multiple parameters that can be set and altered for multiple applications. It is also suitable for repetitive tasks such as the creation of batch files. However, it is more suitable for expert users since it can be frustrating for the novice user given its learning curve. It also has poor error handling and requires substantial training and memorization.

From the EECA perspective, the Command-Line shows that intention formation, specification of the action, and the execution stages are complex. It also, requires a rather accurate mental model of the computer's internal processing. From the Interaction Framework perspective, it translates the user's task language into the input language. It requires knowledge of the core language but the output language can be confusing for inexperienced users since it provides little feedback (Hem 2007).

Menu-Based Interface

Menu-driven interfaces present users with a list of alternatives or options. Textual menus allow menu selection by keying in the number or letter that is associated with that option while graphical menus use arrow keys or pointing devices such as pen or mouse.

Graphical menus can have different forms. Pull down menus provide a vertical list of options to users and cascading menus must be requested by the user from another higher level menu. Some designers use pop-up and iconic menus in order to save screen space.

Menus can be Ideal for novice or intermittent users. However, they can appeal to expert users if display and selection mechanisms are rapid and if appropriate "shortcuts" are implemented. Menus can afford exploration (users can "look around" in the menus for the appropriate command, unlike having to remember the name of a command *and* its spelling when using command language) and allow easy support of error handling as the user's input does not have to be parsed (as with command language) (Preece et al. 1994).

On the other hand, too many menus may lead to information overload or complexity of discouraging proportions. They may be slow for frequent users and may not be suited for small graphic displays (Preece et al. 1994).

From the EEAC perspective, menu constraints can help the user to form the proper intentions and specify the proper action sequence and provide a context to evaluate the output language (Heim 2007).

Form Fill-in

They are used primarily for data entry or data retrieval and they use the computer screen similar to a paper form. Form Fill-ins are similar to menu interfaces in the sense that they present screens of information. However, they are different than menu interfaces since they are used to capture information and proceed linearly instead of navigating a hierarchical structure. The use of form fill-in requires the use of design tools. Heim (2007) and Shneiderman & Plaisant (2005) mention the following advantages and disadvantages with the use of form fill-in:

Forms simplify data entry and require little training compared to other interaction styles such as command lines. They permit the use of form management tools, have low memory requirements and are self-explanatory (Shneiderman & Plaisant 2005).

On the other hand, they require valid input in valid format, require familiarity with interface controls (e.g. Windows), can be difficult to correct mistakes and consume screen space (Shneiderman & Plaisant 2005).

Spreadsheets

These are sophisticated variations of form fill-ins. The first spreadsheet was VISICALC developed by VisiCorp followed by Lotus 1-2-3. Microsoft Excel is the most popular spreadsheet nowadays. The spreadsheet consists of a grid of cells that contain values or formulas. Formulas can involve values of other cells and the user can enter and alter data to the spreadsheet.

Spreadsheets have unlimited space to work with and allow to perform complex calculations. On the other hand, they can be difficult to learn and might require programming skills.

Question and Answer

Question and answer was primarily used to supplement either menu or command line styles. This type of interaction requires that you consider all possible correct answers and deal with the actions to be taken if incorrect answers are entered. Although they are used for mainframe applications, Question and Answer interfaces are more popular in windows applications and normally called wizards. This type of interface is restricting for expert users but ideal for novice users that need to be guided during the interaction process.
This type of interaction has low memory requirements and ideal for applications that are targeted towards beginners. On the other hand, it requires valid input supplied by user and familiarity with interface controls. It can also be very tedious to correct mistakes (Heim 2007).

Direct Manipulation

This interaction style focuses on using icons, or small graphic images, to suggest functions to the user. Today, direct manipulation interaction (Dennehy, 2007) is seamlessly integrated with the menu style since many menus include icons in order to represent menu actions.

From the EEAC perspective, this style offers a wide range of possible intentions. Users usually have multiple options for specifying action sequences. However, the style can be overwhelming for novice users and provide multiple ways of executing action sequences.

With this interaction style, users do not need to remember a command set or recognize commands from menu. The user can easily undo operations and get immediate feedback to his or her actions. On the other hand, infrequent users need to remember the meaning of direct manipulation operations and require interactive devices (e.g., stylus, mouse) in order to manipulate graphical objects in the screen. In addition, this interaction style might require specific computer hardware graphic requirements and take too much space of the screen (Leventhal & Barnes 2007).

Metaphors

Metaphors are visual relationships to real-world objects that are used in interaction design in order to help users relate to complex concepts and procedures. They make learning new systems easier and make computers more accessible to beginner users. In addition, they exploit user's familiar knowledge, helping them to understand the unfamiliar. An example of this is the trash icon in the Windows operating system; this metaphor might symbolize a delete command. Selecting the icon with a pointing device such as a mouse executes the function.

However, the use of metaphors can present problems such as conflicts with design principles. Macintosh thrash has two completely different functions contradicting each other. It served to eject disk as well as delete files. Furthermore, metaphors can be too constraining like in the case of a windows directory that requires the user to scroll through it in order to find a file when it might be easier just to type the name of the file if it is known.

Some other potential problems are identified by Heim (2007) and listed below:
- Run out of metaphors since some virtual processes and objects have no real-world counter parts.
- Mixed metaphors.
- Carry connotations and associations.

Web Navigation

Web navigation has basically two main interaction styles: link-based navigation and search (Heim 2007). The link-based navigation is based on hyperlinks and requires understanding of the hyperlink label or image. This can be problematic since the user might have a different interpretation of the actual meaning of the hyperlink.
The search style minimizes this ambiguity with the help of a search engine that is used to interact with the user. However, the search engine might lead to wrong interpretations if it doesn't take into consideration spelling variations or incorrect search criteria input.

3D Environment

The 3D interaction is natural to most users since it recreates the real-world that can be perceived in a 3D space. This interaction style is popular in computer games but it has the problem of being processor intensive. For this reason, 3D interfaces normally use information in vector based format in order to decrease file sizes and facilitate mathematical calculations required for 3D geometrical transformations used for interface navigation. The basic 3D transformations are scaling, translation and rotation. An overview of these transformations is described by the Weiguang's notes (2007) at http://www.rhpcs.mcmaster.ca/~guanw/course/vis3D.pdf.

Some vector based files used in 3D interfaces include X3-D (Web3D.org) and VRML (Virtual Reality Modeling language). Although 3D interfaces were initially used mainly in computer games, they have been recently used for desktop applications. An example of this effort is the Task Gallery developed by Microsoft. An interesting video that presents this technology can be found at http://research.microsoft.com/ui/TaskGallery/video.mpg.

Zoomable Interface

The zooming interface paradigm (ZIP) was introduced by Raskin (2000). He described the ZIP paradigm by using the concept of ZoomWorld that was based on the idea that the user has access to an infinite plane of information having infinite resolution. The plane is ZoomWorld. Everything the user accesses is displayed somewhere on ZoomWorld, whether it is on a computer, on a local network to which your computer is attached, or on a network of networks, such as the Internet.

In this ZoomWorld, you think of the user as flying higher and higher above it. To look at a particular item, the user dives down to it. ZoomWorld also has a content searching mechanism. The overall metaphor is one of flying, climbing to zoom out and diving to zoom in. The user navigates both by flying above ZoomWorld and by doing content searches.

The ZIP readily permits labels to be attached to images and to collections of images yet does not impose any structure, hierarchical or otherwise, beyond association due to proximity. For example, a large heading Personal Photos might, when zoomed in on, reveal smaller headings on groups of pictures labeled Baby Pictures, Vacations, Pets, Hobbies, Friends, Relatives, and so forth. Zooming in to the writing under the heading Baby Pictures might reveal the children's names.

An interesting zooming user interface (ZUI), called PAD++ (it is now called Jazz), has been developed independently, originally at the University of New Mexico. See http://www.cs.umd.edu/hcil/pad++/.

Natural Language

The natural language relieves the user of the burden of learning syntaxes or getting familiar with graphical objects since it interacts with the user by using everyday language. The style is ideal for users not familiar with computer systems and for hands free and mobile applications. This style uses speech recognition or typed natural language. However, there are problems associated with this style and highlighted by Leventhal & Barnes (2007) and Shneiderman & Plaisant (2005) in the following list:

- It is unpredictable
- May require many keystrokes
- Rigid sequences so user would need to remember sequences
- Typing with an onscreen keyboard could be slow and error prone. No evidence that phone has speech input.
- Recall. Infrequent or new users may have some problems recalling what the inputs should be.
- Vague and ambiguous

Summary

The Execution/Evaluation Action Cycle model was introduced and its usefulness to compare different interaction styles and paradigms highlighted with some examples. The Dix et. al Interaction framework was presented and its use to model interaction operations was discussed. Different interaction styles were covered and their benefits and problems were discussed for different interaction applications.

References

Dennehy, M. 2007, Direct Manipulation. The Encyclopedia of Virtual Environments. Virtual Reality and Telepresence Course, [Online] Available: http http://www.hitl.washington.edu/scivw/EVE/I.D.2.c.DirectManipulation.html [Accessed 20 Nov 2007]

Dix, A., Finlay., Abowd, G., & Beale, R. 1998, *Human-computer interaction*, Prentice Hall, Upper Saddle River, NJ.

Heim, S. 2007, *The resonant interface*, Addison-Wesley, Boston MA.

Leventhal, L. & Barnes, J., 2007, *Usability Engineering*: Process, Products and Examples, Prentice Hall, Upper Saddle River, N.J.

Norman, D. 1983, 'Some Observations on Mental Models', in *Mental Models*, eds Gentner, D. A. & Stevens, A. A. Hillsdale, NJ: Erlbaum.

Norman D. 1998, *The invisible computer*, MIT Press, Cambridge MA.

Norman D. 1990, *The design of everyday things*, Doubleday/Currency, New York.

Preece, J. J., Rogers, Y. R., Sharp, H., Benyon, D. R., Holland, S. and Carey, T. 1994, *Human-Computer Interaction*. Addison-Wesley, New York , N.Y.

Raskin, J. 200, *Human Interface, the: New directions for Designing Interactive designs*, Addison Wesley Professional, New York, N.Y.

Shneiderman, B. 1997, Designing information-abundant web sites: issues and recommendations. In *Web Usability*, eds Buckingham S. & McKnight C., *Int. J. Human-Computer Studies*.

Shneiderman B. & Plaisant S. 2005, *Designing the User Interface*, Peason Education, Reading MA.

Young, R.M. 1983, 'Surrogates and Mappings: two Kinds of Conceptual Models for Interactive Devices'. In *Mental Models*, eds Gentner, D. & Stevens, A. L. Hillsdale, NJ: Erlbaum.

Young, R.M. 1981, 'The Machine Inside the Machine: User's Models of Pocket Calculators'. *International Journal Of Man-Machine Studies*, vol. **15** ,no. 1, pp. 51-85.

Weiguang G. 2007, Course notes in 3D graphics [Online], Available: http://www.rhpcs.mcmaster.ca/~guanw/course/vis3D.pdf, [Accessed 15 Nov 2007]

Discussion questions

6. Choose a few of the possible combinations presented in the table below, for instance, Form Fill-In and Mobile, and write a one-to-two page report on a possible interaction design resulting from the combination. Use the 5W+H heuristic to structure your report and discuss the possible range of tasks that might be supported as well as the hardware that might be involved.

   You should discuss the advantages as well as the disadvantages resulting from the combinations. Consider also the possibility that a particular combination will yield no practical applications; if so, you should articulate the reasons for this determination.

	Large Scale	Mobile	Personal	Networked
Command Line				
Menu				
Form Fill-In				
Question and Answer				
Direct Manipulation				
3-D				
Zoomable				
Natural Language				

7. Choose two different interaction styles and a particular task. For instance, you might choose Direct Manipulation and Question and Answer and then choose the task of setting up an email account. Then, using Norman's Execution/Evaluation Action Cycle, make a detailed report on how the task will be accomplished. This may take the form of a list of actions that occur at each stage of the model.

   After that is complete, discuss and compare the impact each interaction style will have on the successful completion of the task. Refer to the different stages of the EEAC in your discussion.

8. Using Norman's design questions below, discuss a specific interaction devices for a portable MP3 player. The question "how easily can you..." should be answered by describing the actual device and how the interface looks and functions. For instance, the first question "How easily can you determine the function of the device?" should be answered by listing the functions (Execution) and describing how each function is made visible to the user (Evaluation).

   Given a particular interface design, how easily can you; (Norman, 1990)
   - Determine the function of the device?
   - Tell what actions are possible?

- Determine mapping from intention to physical movement?
- Perform the action?
- Tell if system is in the desired state?
- Determine the mapping from system state to interpretation?
- Tell what state the system is in?

9. Now take the same device and discuss its operation in terms of the Interaction Framework of Dix et al.

Activities

Starting with this chapter and continuing through the rest of the book you will be involved in the creation of an interaction design.

The design project can be based on, but is not restricted to, any one of the following interfaces (bear in mind that you need to prototype the interface for this project in future weeks):
- Website
- Kiosk
- Windows Application
- Mobile devices

For this seminar, you will be responsible for the submission of a document with the following components:
- 5W+H heuristic
- Interaction Paradigm
- Physical Computing Environment

Activity sample solution

Interaction Design for an university information website

The marketing department has been given the task of redesigning from scratch a technical university's website in order to raise the public profile of the institution its courses and facilities, and attract more enrolment applications. The logic behind the redesign is that most students "shop around" before making a decision and the convenience of the web means that many if not most will make the choice from the comfort of their homes without ever setting foot on any of the campuses being considered. As such, the Senior Managers have taken a chunk of the budget from the on-campus student information centre and have redirected it to the marketing department for a major "online presence" overhaul. All design elements, content, and functionality must be geared towards the selling of the institution to present and future clients and stakeholders.

A) 5W+H heuristic

What/How *(the physical and virtual interface components. For example, I/O devices, windows, icons, etc.)*

The website will be viewed through a PC or Mac using a standard browser (v4+). Navigation and selection will be performed using a standard mouse and keyboard. Speakers will be necessary to hear some of the animated multimedia presentations contained within some of the pages. Many brochures will be presented for downloading in PDF format: it is assumed that most users will have the option of printing the documentation for reading away from the computer screen.

The different areas of the site will be accessible by;

- A menu based navigation system combining 6 -8 top menu items with submenus of no more than six clickable links that appear in drop down style with the mouseover event.
- A search engine, programmed to perform fuzzy matching with possible misspelled word, and linked to a database of page descriptions

Where/When *(physical environment: the differences between office, portable, wearable systems.)*

The site will be visited by users in a home or work environment, perhaps in preparation for a visit to the campus, or simply to help in the choice of universities and courses. A version of the site will be compatible with smaller mobile devices (iPad and iPhone). The site will be accessible at any time of day. Visit to the site will probably rise during the two major enrollment periods of the year.

Who/Why *(the types of tasks and skill sets required)*

It is expected that the vast majority of visitors will be school leavers, currently enrolled students and the parents or friends of both. The main task set by visitors will concern locating and perhaps printing data that helps them make informed choices about their tertiary studies

B) Interaction Paradigm

Internet/Web based network computing. Graphical and multimedia interface interpreted by a v4++ web browser, delivered over a network to desktop and mobile devices, themselves controlled by either 1) mouse and keyboard or 2) by touch screen and keyboard.

C) Physical Computing Environment

The physical computing environment is, strictly speaking, the 300 million or so personal computers, kiosks and mobile devices that are connected to, and form, the Internet. Since this largest ever engineering feat is spread out geographically and offers content delivery for a variety of output devices and screen sizes, it is not possible to define the physical computing environment as a single, universally shared experience. Users may be sitting on a bus or walking down the street (iPad or iPhone) or at home with a 17 inch screen, at work with a 21-inch screen, or in a public library: the amount of physical space and the quality of the experience depends on the physical environment of each individual user. Typically, the user will be at home, at a workstation that may or may not be cluttered with high school leaving certificate text books.

References
Heim, S. (2008) *The Resonant Interface*. Pearson. Boston, USA.
Laureate Online Education (2008) *HCI: Seminar 2* [Online]

Chapter 3

Discovery methods for HCI

In chapter 3, we will explore the discovery phase framework in HCI for interface requirements definition. Data collection methods will be explored in detail. Task analysis will be covered as the base for requirements discovery. Documentation techniques of HCI requirements will be included in this seminar.

Requirements Discovery phase

Requirements discovery phase includes different techniques to be used by HCI designers to identify interaction requirements from the users of the HCI. As part of this requirements discovery, it is important to learn more about the user in the environment in which he or she would be using the interface. In order to learn about the user, it is important to identify the data collection methods that will be used to gather data that would reveal user's behaviours and preferences.

This data collected needs to be organized and transformed into requirements that can be used for the HCI design. This takes different techniques such as task analysis, use cases, primary stakeholder profile and storyboarding which will be covered in this lecture. The result of this phase is a requirements definition document that balances the needs of the user, the business, and the technical necessities.

Methods of Collection

Data gathering is an important part of the requirements discovery process in interaction design. Data collection includes observation and elicitation methods. Observation methods allow the designer to immerse themselves in users' environment in their day-to-day activity by watching them but users don't participate directly with the HCI designer. On the other hand, elicitation methods require user's participation and include direct and indirect methods such as interviews, focus groups, and questionnaires.

Direct Observation

This occurs when a field visit is conducted during the interaction design. Observation is a requirements discovery technique wherein the HCI designers either participates in or watches a person perform activities to learn about the interaction.

Before observation can be used in discovery, three minimum conditions set out by Tull and Hawkins (1993) need to be met:
- The data has to be available for observation
- The behaviour has to be repetitive, frequent, or otherwise predictable
- An event has to cover a reasonably short time span.

Through observation, it is possible to describe what goes on, who or what is involved, when and where things happen, how they occur, and why things happen as they do in particular situations (Jorgensen 1989). A great deal of time is spent on paying attention, watching and listening carefully (Neuman 1994). The observer uses all the senses, noticing what is seen, heard, smelled, tasted and touched (Neuman 1994; Spradley 1979).

According to Neuman (1994), there are four possible research stances for the participant observer:

- Complete participant: the researcher operates under conditions of secret observation and full participation.
- Complete observer: the researcher is behind a one-way mirror or in an invisible role that permits undetected and unnoticed observation and eavesdropping.
- Participant as observer: the researcher and members are aware of the research role, but the researcher is an intimate friend who is a pseudomember.
- Observer as participant: the researcher is a known, overt observer from the beginning, who has more limited or formal contact with members.

Whitten et. al (2000) suggested the following points when observing in the requirements discovery.

- Determine the who, what, where, when, why, and how of the observation.
- Obtain permission from appropriate supervisors or managers.
- Inform those who will be observed of the purpose of the observation.
- Keep a low profile.
- Take notes during or immediately following the observation.
- Review observation notes with appropriate individuals.
- Don't interrupt the individuals at work.
- Don't focus heavily on trivial activities.
- Don't make assumptions.

Interviews

Interviews are a requirements discovery technique whereby the interaction designer collects information from individuals through face-to-face interaction.

Unstructured and open-ended interviews are with only a general goal or subject in mind and with few, if any, specific questions. The interviewer counts on the interviewee to provide a framework and direct the conversation.

The goal is to elicit the respondent's views and experiences in his or her own terms, rather than to collect data that are simply a choice among pre-established response categories (Anderson et al. 1994). Secondly, the interview is not bound to a rigid interview format or set of questions that would be difficult to establish given the nature of the research and will limit the results (Anderson et al. 1994).

In structured and close-ended interviews the interviewer has a specific set of questions to ask of the interviewee. Closed-ended questions restrict answers to either specific choices or short, direct responses.

Whitten et. al (2000) suggested the following list of activities that could be used when preparing interviews:

1. Select Interviewees
2. Prepare for the Interview with specific questions the interviewer will ask the interviewee.
3. Conduct the Interview
4. Follow Up on the Interview

Questions should not be leading or loaded. It is important to use consice and clear language and avoid any bias as an interviewer. Keep the questions short and to the point and avoid any intimidating questions.

Focus Groups

Focus groups are a process whereby highly structured group meetings are conducted for the purpose of analyzing problems and defining requirements. Focus groups are a subset of a more comprehensive joint application development or JAD technique that encompasses the entire systems development process.

Focus groups require a facilitator role. Facilitators encourage user and management participation without allowing individuals to dominate the session. They make sure that attendees abide by the established ground rules for the session, encourage group consensus and keep the session on schedule.

Focus groups actively involve users in the interaction design and this improves their acceptance and reduces the risk of resistance at the implementation stage. They reduce the amount of time required to design interactions.

Brainstorming

It is similar to focus group but more informal and use for generating ideas during group meetings. Participants are encouraged to generate as many ideas as possible in a short period of time without any analysis until all the ideas have been exhausted.

Questionnaires

Questionnaires are special-purpose documents that allow the interaction designer to collect information and opinions from respondents. Questionnaires can be in a free or fixed format. Free-format questionnaires offer the respondent greater latitude in the answer. A question is asked, and the respondent records the answer in the space provided after the question. Fixed-format questionnaires contain questions that require selection of predefined responses from individuals and are normally composed of multiple-choice, rating or ranking questions.

Whitten et. al (2000) proposed the following activities when performing data collection with the use of questionnaires.

1. Determine what facts and opinions must be collected and from whom you should get them.
2. Based on the needed facts and opinions, determine whether free- or fixed-format questions will produce the best answers.
3. Write the questions.
4. Test the questions on a small sample of respondents.
5. Duplicate and distribute the questionnaire.

Data collected needs to be interpreted in order to identify the requirements for the design of the HCI. The following tools will be covered for data interpretation:

1. Task analysis
2. Ishikawa diagram
3. Use cases
4. Story boarding
5. Primary stakeholder profiles

Task Analysis

A task is as a set of activities that change the system from an initial state to a specified goal or desired outcome state. The outcome may involve a significant change to the current state, so we split tasks into a sequence of subtasks, each more simple than the parent task. This process continues until the most primitive subtask is reached. This lowest level subtask is variously referred to as an action, simple task, or unit task. Task descriptions are often used to envision new systems or devices

Task analysis is used mainly to investigate an existing situation. It is used to determine functionality by distinguishing the tasks and subtasks performed. Particular attention is paid to frequent tasks, occasional tasks, exceptional tasks, and errors. Identifying goals and the strategies (combinations of tasks) used to reach those goals is also part of a good task analysis. By conducting a task analysis, the designer learns about the sequences of events that a user may experience in reaching a goal (Diaper 1989).

Rees et al. (2001) propped a list of activities in order to conduct task analysis and are described below:

1. Gathering information from observation of and/or consulting with users
2. Representing tasks in a task description notation
3. Performing an analysis of the task descriptions to achieve an optimum description
4. Using the task representation to produce a new user interface design or improve an existing one

The most popular technique used for this type of analysis is the Hierarchical Task Analysis (HTA) tool. It involves breaking a task down into subtasks, then sub-sub-tasks and so on. These are grouped as plans which specify how the tasks might be performed in practice. It focuses on physical and observable actions and includes looking at actions not related to software or an interaction device. Start with a user goal which is examined and the main tasks for achieving it are identified.

In order to demonstrate the use of HTA, let's use an example of a task analysis for borrowing a book from the library. The set of tasks and subtasks for borrowing the book from the library is presented in figure 1.

1. Walk to the library
2. Search for the book
        2.1 Access the library's catalogue computer system

2.2 Access the search book screen
2.3 Enter the in the search criteria the book title and author
2.4 Locate required book
2.5 Take note of the book's location
3   Walk to the book's location
4   Take the book and walk to the checkout counter

Figure 1 HTA for borrowing the book from the library

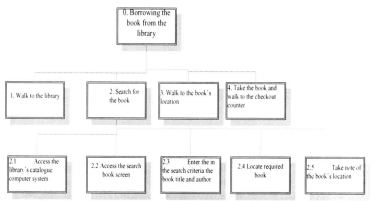

Figure 2 Graphical HTA for borrowing the book from the library

More examples on how to use this tool can be found in Hierarchical Task Analysis links section at the end of this lecture.

Ishikawa diagram

The Ishikawa diagram is a graphical tool used to identify, explore, and depict problems and the causes and effects of those problems. It is often referred to as a cause-and-effect diagram or a fishbone diagram. This tool is used by designers in order to identify problems with the interaction that could be tackled with the new design.

An overview of this tool and examples can be seen at
http://www.mindtools.com/pages/article/newTMC_03.htm.

Use Cases

One of the most popular and successful approaches for documenting business processes, events and responses is a technique called *use cases* developed by Dr. Ivar Jacobson (Jacobson et al. 1993). Use cases describe the business process, and document how the business works and the business goals of each interaction with the system. These use cases are then extended to show how the human interaction will support the business goals.

The interactions within the use case should be contained, initiated and seen through to completion by an actor. The use case should further result in achieving a business goal and leaving the system in a stable state (Reed 2002). The nature of a use case is to define the *"what"* of a system.

An actor represents anything that needs to interact with the system to exchange information. An actor is a user, a role, which could be an external system as well as a person.

Benefits of use cases are highlighted by Witthen et. al (2000):

- Facilitates user involvement.
- A view of the desired human interaction's functionality from an external person's viewpoint.
- An effective tool for validating requirements.
- An effective communication tool.

A good example on how to document HCI requirements by using use cases can be found at http://genben.com/haojie/HCI/HCI_Requirements.doc.

Storyboards

Movies studios create storyboards that show the various scenes of a potential film, particularly an animated film. A storyboard puts ideas on paper and then puts the papers in a certain sequence to provide a concept of how the film will play out. It also gives the production team an opportunity to look at the concept and make suggestions for improving the film before it takes its final form.

In user interface design, there is a more interactive version of storyboarding called paper prototyping. Paper prototyping involves creating a paper version of a software program, hardware product, or Web site so you can learn how users interact with the design before you develop the product. This paper prototype involves using a series of images that can be animated, used to describe a work flow for a human computer interaction. They can facilitate the process of task decomposition and the identification of interface requirements since they help to visualize existing work flows.

A good article about paper prototyping can be found at http://www.uie.com/articles/paper_prototyping/.

Primary Stakeholder Profiles

The HCI design includes four distinct stakeholder groups (Donoghue, 2002):

- Users
- Engineers and designers
- Sales and marketing personnel
- Managers

Users are the primary stakeholders since the use the design directly. Engineers and designers are secondary stakeholders since they supply input or receive output for the design. Managers are facilitators since they help to maintain the design. Sales and marketing personal are indirect stakeholders since they are affected by the design but they don't have direct contact with it. Users expect to have a successful experience with the user interface (UI) the first time around. Because the users are the people who determine whether something is useful, the characteristics of your users will go a long way toward determining what is actually usable. However, users look for some general goals when they use an interface (Donoghue, 2002):

- The UI must be easy to learn.
- The UI must solve the user's needs.
- The UI help must be both easily accessible and effective in resolving the user's problem quickly.

Defining a user's profile is an essential prerequisite for designing a HCI. The user profile will influence the design and evaluation of an interface. Badre (2002) suggested the following activities to generate a user profile:

1. Identify the relevant individual differences.
2. Identify and specialize the cognitive processing capabilities and limits.
3. Generate audience definition and categorization.

Individual differences can be grouped into four categories (Badre 2002):

1. Knowledge, experience, and skill: Individual users may differ in level and type of education as well as in their knowledge, experience, and skill levels. There are several key factors in this category that are determinants of a user's performance. These factors describe the cognitive abilities and styles of projected users as well as their knowledge and experience of the projected HCI's domain.
2. Personality factors: Affect the ease of user acceptance for interacting with and navigating a HCI. Such attributes as tolerance level and motivation should indicate how much time users will spend trying to use the new HCI to perform a transaction before giving up.
3. Physical and demographic attributes: Demographic attributes with implications for the design of a HCI are age, gender, salary, and mobility. An audience definition statement should take into account factors related to physical capabilities and limitations. Issues that might affect design include the use of glasses (nearsightedness, bifocals), left- and right-handedness, auditory devices, and other visual and motor aids.
4. User levels: The designer should take into consideration the users' varying levels of expertise with the computing environment used for the HCI. Level can range from novice to master level.

The usability effectiveness of designs depends in great part on their compatibility with the user's information-processing capabilities and limitations. Designers must take into account the users' cognitive and perceptual limits and how people are likely to process information in an interactive environment. There are some basic universal human information-processing characteristics, which affect the way people store, remember, and manipulate information, which in turn have implications for HCI design. For example, if the user has selective attention, this means both creating designs that draw user attention to a particular screen location and optimizing the ease of locating displayed information such as using a unique bright color to draw attention to a displayed link can increase the chances that it will be noticed before other links.

Generating an audience profile means generating a document that specifies the relevant characteristics, the range and frequency values of the identified characteristics, and how this specified information might impact design decisions.

User profiles can be also seen from the marketing point of view. Eisenberg and Eisenberg (2006) discussed the creation of primary stakeholder profiles in terms of marketing, which essentially means to persuade the user that the interface is worth using. Profiles connect three different dimensions of information:

- Demographics: This segments some of the persona features. For example, demographic data shows such data as the user's gender, location, and income.
- Psychographics: This segments some of the persona needs and determines questions that each persona may ask. For example, a spontaneous type and a competitive type will ask different questions and will want different types of information.
- Topology: This allows you to segment by determining how complex the persuasion process is; that complexity is based on a customer's perceptions and experiences.

Regarding the topology dimension, Eisenberg and Eisenberg mapped a four-dimension model for the process of persuasion in sales:

- Need: This is the urgency that a user feels for a product or service.
- Risk: This is the amount of risk the user is willing to accept regarding such features as a career or self-esteem.
- Knowledge: This is how much knowledge the user has about the product, which can affect need and risk. For example, if someone feels he doesn't have enough information about a product or service, the risk factor for that user is higher.
- Consensus: This is the understanding during the persuasion process of how many people need to be convinced and when.

Marketing analysis and existing competition

Marketing plays an important role when defining HCI requirements. Designers need to take into consideration competition and existing technologies when defining requirements in order to build competitive interactions. Users are driving the marketing and acceptance of user interfaces therefore it is important to make every effort to find out market demographics. A marketing analysis for defining requirements of the HCI can be done by using the techniques suggested by Cooper and Reimann (2003):

- Reviews of competing products.
- Reviews of market research, such as computing media Web sites and technology white papers.
- Researching market demographics in the area that the HCI will be used. That research can include analyzing demographic, geographic, or behavioral variables to see if any patterns emerge.

29

Documenting HCI requirements

Requirements need to be documented after they are discovered by the HCI designer. A requirements definition document should consist of the following according to Whitten et al. (2000):

1. The functions and services the system should provide.
2. Nonfunctional requirements including the system's features, characteristics, and attributes.
3. The constraints that restrict the development of the system or under which the system must operate.
4. Information about other systems the system must interface with.

Heim (2007) proposes that the formal discovery documentation should include:

1. Mission Statement
2. Requirements Document
3. Project Management Document
4. Usability Guidelines

Summary

The discovery of requirements phase was defined and the different components required to discover requirements were included in this lecture. The observation and elicitation data collection methods used in the discovery phase were explained in the context of HCI. Data interpretation mechanisms were covered and included task analysis, ishikawa diagrams, use cases, story boarding and primary stakeholder profiles. Marketing analysis as a baseline to develop competitive HCI designs was emphasized. The main components when documenting HCI requirements were highlighted and discussed.

References

Anderson, J.G., Aydin, C. E., & Jay, S. J. 1994, *Evaluating Health Care Information Systems: Methods and Applications*. Sage publications, USA.

Badre, A. 2003, *Shaping Web Usability: Interaction Design in Context*, Addison Wesley Professional.

Bell, J. 1992, *Doing your research project*, Milton Keynes: Open University Press, UK.

Benbasat, I., Goldstein, D. & Mead, M. 1987, 'The Case Research Strategy in Studies of Information Systems', MIS Quarterly, vol.11, no.3, pp 368-386

Cooper, A. & Reimann, R. 2003, *About Face 2.0*,Wiley Publishing, Indianapolis, IN.

Diaper, D. 1989, *Task Analysis for Human-Computer Interaction*. Hillsdale, Chichester, UK, Ellis Horwood.

Donoghue, K. 2002, *Built for Use*, McGraw-Hill, New York.

Eisenberg, B. & Eisenberg, J. 2006, *Waiting for Your Cat to Bark?,* Thomas Nelson, Inc. Nashville, TN.

Heim, S. 2007, *The resonant interface,* Addison-Wesley, Boston MA.

Rees, M., White, A. & Bebo, W. 2001, *Designing Web Interfaces*, Prentice Hall.

Reed, Jr, P.R. 2002, *Developing Applications with JAVA and UML*, Addison-Wesley, Boston.

Stake, R.E. 1995, *The art of case study research,* Sage publishing, California, CA.

Jacobson, I., Christerson, M., Jonsson, P. & Overgaard, G. 1993, *Object-oriented Software Engineering: A Use Case Driven Approach*, Addison-Wesley, Wokingham, Englad.

Jorgensen, D. L. 1989, *Participant observation: Methodology for human studies*, Sage publications, Newbury, CA.

Tull, D. and Hawkins, D. 1993, *Marketing Research: Measurement and Method*, Macmillan Publishing Company, New York, NY.

Neuman, W.L. 1994, *'Sampling', in Social Research Methods*, Allyn and Bacon, Boston.

Whitten, J. L., Bentley D. L. & Dittman K.V. 2000, *Systems Analysis and Design Methods*, McGraw-Hill, New York

Discussion questions

1. Choose a task that involves multiple people and provide a use case for the task. This may be something that is performed at work or in an academic department. It must be large enough to provide an opportunity to create the Use Case.

2. Discuss some of the ways users can be involved in the design process.

3. Compare and contrast the methods used for observation and elicitation. Discuss what they are best suited for, when they should be applied and what results can be expected.

4. Choose three typical computing tasks that you perform regularly. Provide a Task Decomposition for each task and then provide an HTA of these same tasks.

Activities

For this chapter, you will continue with your interaction design project. You will be responsible for the submission of a document that defines the following discovery activities:

- The project stakeholders
  - Primary
  - Secondary
  - Facilitator
  - Indirect
- Marketing analysis and existing competition
- The methods of data collection that will be used to discover requirements and all documents required to perform the observations and/or elicitations (questionnaires, surveys etc.)
- Documents pertaining to the interpretation activities. Given the time constraints, you will not be able to execute your data collection plan so in this section you should describe (in general) the expected users, their work contexts, and what they will use the envisaged HCI for with the help of the tools below.
  - Task Analysis
  - Use Cases
- Tentative list of requirements. In this section, you will be required to create a tentative list of requirements based on your task analysis and use cases. From the task analysis and use cases, extract the major HCI requirements and prioritize them into a) absolutely must include; b) should include; and c) could include. Each category should be accompanied by a discussion as to why items were placed in that category.

Activities sample solution

The marketing department has been given the task of redesigning from scratch a technical university's website in order to raise the public profile of the institution its courses and facilities, and attract more enrolment applications. All design elements, content, and functionality must be geared towards the selling of the institution to present and future clients and stakeholders.

The project stakeholders

The following stakeholders will be called upon for authorisation, input or feedback during the design process, including usability testing, and also for a period to be defined after the live launch.

• Primary

The primary stakeholders in the website. The users, namely

• Secondary

The engineers and designers, namely

• Facilitator

The managers

• Indirect

Sales and marketing personnel

Marketing analysis and existing competition

a) The methods of data collection that will be used to discover requirements

- **Research by websites of competitors**

Online research coupled with a checklist of features to be filled out while surfing

- **Questionnaires**
  Especially for research into the demographics of these future users (gender, location, income, interests). Questionnaires will be aimed at eliciting behavioral and demographic information about users based on existing first year candidates. Question should include level of accessibility to internet in the home, the type of screen and browser used, as well as questions about the ease and comfort of surfing the web, which would include questions about family size, where the computer is located and if printer access is easy (many of the students applying come from very large families where an uninterrupted and comfortable website experience may not be possible, even if the household is well-equipped technologically)

- **Focus groups/ Brainstorming**
With representative from all stakeholder groups

- **Interviews**
  Interviews with marketing department, student services, curriculum unit, student representatives "What could the website do to attract the interest of high school leavers and other candidates for enrollment?"

- **Direct observation**
Preferably conducted on campus using visitors to the student information centre selected at random and asked to use the website to accomplish a set of predefined tasks. Preference will be given to users who have not as yet seen the website

b) **all documents required to perform the observations and/or elicitations (questionnaires, surveys etc.)**
Forms will be designed to collect feedback. Some will be online and collaborative, for example the feedback from existing staff members will be placed on the University's intranet and allow for editing:

Name	Faculty/Department	Feedback, Alterations, Suggestions
John Doe	Marketing & Liaison	On all pages where we talk about application fees – the fee should be clearly indicated to avoid the impression that it is free.

Other forms will be on paper, either for direct filling out by stakeholders, or for recording data during interviews
The expected users
The targeted users are young Bahraini school leavers, both male and female, who have experience using the internet to find answer to their questions. They are acquainted with up to date computer graphic designs and are not easily impressed. However, they may not have state of the art printers, screens or PCs so care should be taken to avoid slowness of downloaded elements (e.g. a 6MB PDF is to be avoided if at all possible). They have many different personality types though will all share a desire to pursue studies that are interesting, fun, in an environment that they will find stimulating both intellectually and socially, and enrolled in a programme that is likely to lead them to a well paid and interesting job upon graduation. Most of them will be in the middle of their final school exams and would enjoy a website experience that lifts them out of pre-exam stress, promising a type of learning environment that is mercifully different from their current high-school. Many will see entry into a university degree programme as a rite of passage, a first taste of adulthood and greater freedom. All of these factors must be impressed on the technicians and graphic designers of the future website.

• **Task Analysis**

Task: obtaining a paper version of a degree programme booklet
1   Go onto university website
2   Search for the desired programme
2.1   Access the search engine of tree menu under Programmes/Courses
2.2   Select the desired programme
2.3   Scroll down to printer icon for booklet
3   Click on link to printer friendly or PDF version of booklet
4   Go to printer and staple pages together

• **Use Cases**

Use cases will be created to analyse current business processes with a view to taking some if not all of the interactions onto the website. Certain issues may surround the creation of online versions for the taking of ID photos or the paying administrative costs, and they will have to be weighed for pros and cons.
The example case will be: Applying in person for enrolment at the university. The actors are:
a) Future Student (hereafter: Student)
b) Clerk 1
c) Cashier
Steps/Phases in the Use Case:
1. Student goes to website for list of necessary documents
Student needs to ensure that the visit to the university will not be a waste of time. This means that research needs to be done into the eligibility of the student for entry into a programme , ensuring that an exhaustive list of necessary documents is known ahead of time so that a key item is not missing, thus making the process unable to be completely performed. The website will provide a map and instructions how to get there
2. **Prepare documents**: ID, school record etc
3. **Go to Student service centre reception** and take a ticket and wait for number to come up on electronic display. The main point of entry is where Student explains purpose of visit and is directed to the appropriate room for processing
4. Go to desk number 1 and **ask for form to full out:** After waiting for number to appear, final verification of eligibility based on nationality and academic record is confirmed and clerk checks that Student has all necessary items for complete processing. In case of missing items Student is directed to coin operated photocopier. In case of absence of key document like ID, Student is told to return at later date equipped with said documents
5. **Fill in form:** using a pen, Student provided all required information (contact details, resident permit number, student records etc)
6. Student returns to desk 1 (without having to take another number) and **hand over completed form**, photo, and copies of documents
7. **Payment**: Student takes form and bill print out to cashier and pay.
8. **Student goes to waiting room** and waits for name to be called
11. Clerk 1 finishes processing and uses computer program to **generate an official receipt of application form**. Clerk 1 signals to Student that receipt is ready
12. Student Go to desk and **picks up receipt.**

Tentative list of requirements.

1.   **The functions and services the system should provide.**

The site must (absolutely) provide:
- as much information about the university as possible, all in a clear and easy to read format
- clearly indicated access to printer friendly versions of information
- easy to fill in online data collection forms with instant feedback

- payment system built into the application for enrolment section for those wishing to settle application fees by credit card
- online versions of processes that currently require a candidate to visit the University in person. This will require analyses of existing tasks that have the potential to become online applications. For example the current process for inquiring as to eligibility could be transformed into a Wizard-like interaction style based on the following flow chart:

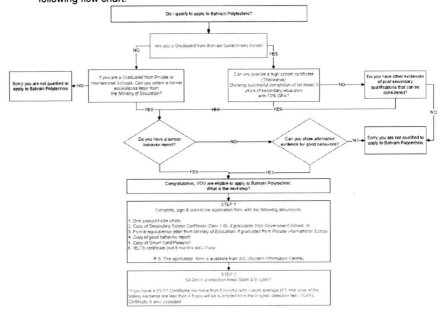

2. Nonfunctional requirements including the system's features, characteristics, and attributes.

The system should include easy to access information about:
- Eligibility for enrolment
- How to enrol
- The programmes on offer
- Student life
- Address
- Job Vacancies
- How to get there by various means of transport
- Address and contact information
- University mission statement

3. The constraints that restrict the development of the system or under which the system must operate.

There will be the usual constraints linked to development of any website, namely, the use of large graphic files should be limited to allow for shorter download time and ease of navigation. Users will spend on average three seconds waiting for a page to load: beyond that, they are likely to leave the site and check the competitor's website. It is likely that school leavers will not all have fast broadband connections. What graphic designers and animators consider to be a major selling point (i.e. impressive displays of Photoshop or animation dexterity) could in fact prove detrimental to the well-being of the site and therefore the institution. Design and development tricks should be used to create an attractive interface that is fast loading. This will involve the deliberate choice of elements that can be recycled as objects.

4.   Information about other systems the system must interface with.
The website must be integrated with certain existing systems and become the launch pad for interrelated online activities. The will be a portal dimension to the website, with quick links offered to authorized users to the university's intranet, including Learning Management system like Moodle and a campus management system like Banner (Oracle) all operating on different servers

Chapter 4

Interface and interaction design

In chapter 4, we will learn the user-centered design paradigm. Interaction design models are introduced. Interface design standards, conceptual design and design principles are included. Interface components as windows, icons, menus and pointers and other components will be included in this chapter.

Conceptual Design

After the requirements discovery phase is completed, the design phase uses the requirements in order to create conceptual and physical designs. In this lecture, the conceptual design will be covered in detail.

Conceptual design is the creation of alternative design ideas. At this stage, a description of the proposed system is presented in terms of a set of integrated ideas and concepts about what it should do, behave and look like.

The conceptual design follows requirements analysis but precedes the physical design. It helps to determine functions, operations and features and the workflow of the interface. It also allows the designer to identify inputs and outputs and the style of the interaction.

Several tools for conceptual design will be introduced here including brainstorming, card sort, personas, scenarios, semantic networks and cognitive walkthroughs.

Brainstorming

These are sessions with your project team that will help to uncover ideas that your team can implement now or sometime later. Brainstorming sessions should be centered on a topic. For example, a brainstorming session can center on what user interface elements will meet specific goals. (Cooper & Reimann 2003)

Participants are encouraged to generate as many ideas as possible in a short period of time without any analysis until all the ideas have been exhausted.

Card sort

Card sorting is normally performed with the use of small paper cards that are usually lined. Each card represents one screen and these cards can be shown easily on a table or the wall in order to represent multiple screens. Thread or lines within the cards indicate sequences or hyperlinks. They are used often in web design but can also be used in any design that involves multiple screens.

Card sorting is an excellent way to explore work flow without having to create a detailed screen design. However, they have limitations since it is hard to explore elements that are not included in the cards such as icons or other interface elements.

Scenarios

37

Scenarios can be used to express proposed or imagined situations that describe the different tasks a person would need to do in order to accomplish a specific goal with the design. They are used throughout the design process as scripts for user evaluation of prototypes and for co-operation among designers involved in an interaction project.

In creating such scenarios, a designer specifies interface objects and actions for given contexts from the perspective of the user (Badre 203).

To create successful scenarios, Badre (2002) suggested to answer the following questions.

1. Where and under what conditions will the system be used?
2. For what purpose will the system be used?
3. Who will use the system (the target audience)?
4. How will the system be used?

Scenarios provide a fast and effective way to imagine the design concepts in use. They are simple stories about what it would be like to use the interface once it has been made and the protagonists of these stories are the personas (Saffer 2006).

Semantic Networks

Semantic networks are an excellent way to represent concepts associations in interaction design. Rees et. al (2001) mentioned that the human thought is basically nonlinear and that the human learning and perceptual process is essentially organized as a semantic network in which concepts are linked together by associations. In few words, human learn and remember through nonlinear associations. The fundamental components of a semantic network are:

- Nodes: Representing concepts
- Links: Representing the relationships between nodes.

In a semantic network a node is defined as a single concept or idea. Nodes can be virtually any kind of information such as text, graphics, animation, audio, video, images, programs, and so on. Nodes can be "typed," indicating how they are used. For example, if a node in a Web-based hypertext system is designated as the "home page," there is the implication that that node will be used in a specific way to traverse that system (i.e., it is the node where readers will begin).

Nodes are connected to other nodes with links. The role of a link is to connect related concepts or nodes. Links are bidirectional, meaning that a reader can go backwards and forwards.

Like nodes, links can also be "typed," illustrating features of the relationship of the nodes they connect. For example, a link might reflect some relationship between nodes such as parent–child. (Rees et. al 2001).

A tool that might help in organizing a semantic network (or a brainstorming session) is Free mind (http://freemind.sourceforge.net/wiki/index.php/Main_Page).

Cognitive walkthrough

Cognitive walkthrough is a technique that involves a group of users that evaluates a human interaction by going through a set of tasks. The user interface is presented as a paper prototype to the evaluators and they follow the various scenarios of the interaction. The input to the walkthrough includes the user profile, especially the users' knowledge of the task domain and of the interface, and the task cases. The evaluators may include human factors engineers, software developers, or people from marketing, documentation, etc.

Zhang (2008) identifies the following questions required to design the walkthrough:

- Who will be the users of the system?
- What task(s) will be analyzed?
- What is the correct action sequence for each task?
- How is the interface defined?

Dix et. al (1998) mention that for each task in the walkthrough the evaluator should consider:

- What impact will interaction have on user?
- What cognitive processes are required?
- What learning problems may occur?
- Does the design lead the user to generate the correct goals?

Personas

Personas are profiles of the users that interact with a HCI These profiles describe user characteristics such as user expertise, user motivation, user job functions and the impact of the interaction in the user's job. They help the designer to understand who will be using the interaction in order meet user expectations.

Personas can be created by observing and talking to users. Personas don't have to be for a specific individual but for a set of people that share the same goals. Personas should identify each persona's desires and the expectations, behaviors, attitudes, biases, and other factors that affect them.

A set questions that could be helpful to create a persona are identified by Hackos and Redish (1998) as follows:

- Do you like your work? Why or why not?
- What motivates you in your job?
- Is the database product related directly to your primary job? That is, do you need to use this product every day to get your job done?
- How much do you know about the subject matter you're designing for?
- What technical skills and job knowledge do you bring to the job?

- How do you approach technology? Do you love it or put up with it?
- Do you prefer learning from written documentation, or do you prefer online help? What do you think of the documentation of the current system?
- Do you like new experiences, or do you think if it isn't broken you shouldn't fix it?

Personas might use construct context scenarios that describe personas and their activities in a typical day using the new and improved system, which includes the new user interface. The scenarios don't discuss the form and function, but only the behaviors of the user and the interface (Buttow 2007).

Interaction design models

Interaction design models are useful for analyzing and understanding interface design. They are used to test designs that might be hard to test with real users and prototypes. They can also be used to document designs. Interaction design models can be predictive or descriptive. Predictive models can be used to simulate user actions in order to test a design. Descriptive models are mainly use to document designs and to visualize its logic and behaviour.

In this lecture the GOMS and Keyboard Level Model (KLM) predictive models will be introduced. In addition, the state transition and windows navigation diagrams will be covered as a way to document interactions.

GOMS

The model of goals, operators, methods, and selection rules (GOMS) (Card, Moran, and Newell 1983) allows to predict how long an experienced worker will take to perform a particular operation when using a given interface design.

The significance of these model components is:

- Goals: Symbolic structures that define states to be achieved, and determine a set of possible methods.
- Operators: Elementary motor or information processing acts, whose execution is necessary to change any aspect of the user's memory or to affect the task environment.
- Methods: Descriptions of procedures for accomplishing a goal, cast as a continual sequence of subgoals and operators, with conditional tests on the user's immediate memory and on the task state.
- Selection rules: Elements that allow a choice between two or more methods that can be used to accomplish the goal.

The GOMS models describes the interaction as a sequence of small, discrete subtasks or unit tasks. In order to understand this model, an example of a GOMS model for the task of iconizing a window in an interaction is presented in table 1.

```
GOAL: ICONISE-WINDOW

.  [select GOAL: USE-CLOSE-METHOD

        .  MOVE-MOUSE-TO-WINDOW-HEADER

        .  POP-UP-MENU

        .  CLICK-OVER-CLOSE-OPTION

    GOAL: USE-L7-METHOD

        .  PRESS-L7-KEY]
```

Table 1 GOMS model for iconizing a window

In the model, goals and subgoals are described on bulleted lines, the number of bullets representing the level of subtask. The model includes the concept of selections that represents, at the unit task level, the concept that a user often has a choice of actions. Operators are identified in the description of each task. In the case of the example below, the GOMS model describes that the user can iconize the application by using the use-close or L7 method.

Another example is included in table 2. This example models the task of moving text in a Word processor, in the context of editing a manuscript and is taken from John & Kieras (2006):

```
GOAL: EDIT-MANUSCRIPT
.    GOAL: EDIT-UNIT-TASK ... repeat until no more unit tasks
.  .    GOAL: ACQUIRE UNIT-TASK
.  .            .        GOAL: GET-NEXT-PAGE ... if at end of manuscript page
.  .            .        GOAL: GET-FROM-MANUSCRIPT
.  .        GOAL: EXECUTE-UNIT-TASK ... if a unit task was found
.  .            .        GOAL: MODIFY-TEXT
.  .            .      . [select: GOAL: MOVE-TEXT* ...if text is to be moved
.  .            .        .  GOAL: DELETE-PHRASE ...if a phrase is to be deleted
.  .            .        .  GOAL: INSERT-WORD] ... if a word is to be inserted
.  .            .      . VERIFY-EDIT

*Expansion of MOVE-TEXT goal
GOAL: MOVE-TEXT
.    GOAL: CUT-TEXT
.  .    GOAL: HIGHLIGHT-TEXT
.  .            .        [select**: GOAL: HIGHLIGHT-WORD
.  .            .                     . MOVE-CURSOR-TO-WORD
.  .            .                     . DOUBLE-CLICK-MOUSE-BUTTON
.  .            .                     . VERIFY-HIGHLIGHT
.  .            .                   GOAL: HIGHLIGHT-ARBITRARY-TEXT
.  .            .                     .  MOVE-CURSOR-TO-BEGINNING       1.10
.  .            .                     .  CLICK-MOUSE-BUTTON             0.20
.  .            .                     .  MOVE-CURSOR-TO-END             1.10
```

				SHIFT-CLICK-MOUSE-BUTTON	0.48
				VERIFY-HIGHLIGHT]	1.35
. .		GOAL: ISSUE-CUT-COMMAND			
. .		.	MOVE-CURSOR-TO-EDIT-MENU		1.10
. .		.	PRESS-MOUSE-BUTTON		0.10
. .		.	MOVE-CURSOR-TO-CUT-ITEM		1.10
. .		.	VERIFY-HIGHLIGHT		1.35
. .		.	RELEASE-MOUSE-BUTTON		0.10
.	GOAL: PASTE-TEXT				
. .		GOAL: POSITION-CURSOR-AT-INSERTION-POINT			
. .			MOVE-CURSOR-TO-INSERTION-POIONT		1.10
. .			CLICK-MOUSE-BUTTON		0.20
. .			VERIFY-POSITION		1.35
. .			GOAL: ISSUE-PASTE-COMMAND		
. .			.	MOVE-CURSOR-TO-EDIT-MENU	1.10
. .			.	PRESS-MOUSE-BUTTON	0.10
. .			.	MOVE-MOUSE-TO-PASTE-ITEM	1.10
. .			.	VERIFY-HIGHLIGHT	1.35
. .			.	RELEASE-MOUSE-BUTTON	0.10
				TOTAL TIME PREDICTED (SEC) 14.38	

Table 2 GOMS model for moving text in a Word Processor (John & Kieras 2006)

In this example, the GOMS model includes the time breakdowns for goals and subgoals. This allows goals and subgoals to be measured and likely user performance predicted. For the example presented based on the above GOMS analysis, it should take 14.38 seconds to move text.

Keystroke-Level Model

The Keystroke-Level Model is a simplified version of GOMS and was proposed by Card, Moran & Newell (1980) as a method for predicting user performance. The model is based on the concept that the time that it takes the user-computer system to perform a task is the sum of the times it takes for the system to perform the serial elementary gestures that the task comprises. Although different users might have widely varying times, the researchers found that for many comparative analyses of tasks involving use of a keyboard and a graphical input device, it is possible to use a set of typical times rather than measuring the times of individuals. By means of careful laboratory experiments, Card, Moran and Newell (1983) developed a set of timings for different operations. The model includes six operations including keystroking, pointing, homing, mental preparation and response. The times for these operations are summarized in table 3 below:

K = 0.2 sec	Keying: The time it takes to tap a key on the keyboard
P = 1.1 sec	Pointing: The time it takes a user to point to a position on a display
H = 0.4 sec	Homing: The time it takes a user's hand to move from the keyboard to the GID or from the GID to the keyboard
M = 1.35 sec	Mentally preparing: The time it takes a user

	to prepare mentally for the next step
R	Responding: The time a user must wait for a computer to respond to input

Table 3 Times for the KLM model operations

An example to demonstrate this model is presented in table 4 and borrowed from Hochstein (2003). This example considers the text editing task of searching a Microsoft Word document for all occurrences of a four-letter word, and replacing it with another four-letter word. In the table below, operations are sometimes concantenated and repeated. For example, M4K means Mental preparation, then 4 Key presses."

Description	Operation	Time (sec)
Reach for mouse	H[mouse]	0.40
Move pointer to "Replace" button	P[menu item]	1.10
Click on "Replace" command	K[mouse]	0.20
Home on keyboard	H[keyboard]	0.40
Specify word to be replaced	M4K[word]	2.15
Reach for mouse	H[mouse]	0.40
Point to correct field	P[field]	1.10
Click on field	K[mouse]	0.20
Home on keyboard	H[keyboard]	0.40
Type new word	M4K[word]	2.15
Reach for mouse	H[mouse]	0.40
Move pointer on Replace-all	P[replace-all]	1.10
Click on field	K[mouse]	0.20
Total		**10.2**

Table 3 KLM model for Microsoft Word document for all occurrences of a four-letter word (Hochstein (2002))

State transition diagrams

State transition diagrams are used to model the details of user-computer interaction at the automation level. State transition diagrams can be modeled with the use of UML state charts. The idea of the model is to represent the actions of a finite state machine with no state memory. This processor may be in only one state at a time. A transition to a different state is caused by an event or by a condition's becoming true. Components of a state transition diagram are:

- State: where   the   processor   waits   for an occurrence to cause a transition
- Transition: an instantaneous change to another state

Transitions are labeled to show:
- the event(s) which trigger them, and
- the action(s) occurring during the transition.

43

An event may be constrained by a guard that a condition which must be true for the transition to occur. Figure 1 shows a partial state transition diagram for the interaction design of a CD player. In the diagram is possible to see the events that allow the user to navigate from one state to another. For example, if the user presses the play button, the CD will start playing and remain in a play state. From the play state, it is possible to stop the CD player if the stop button is pressed and go to the stopped state. From the play state is possible to pause the CD player if the pause button is pressed and go to the paused state.

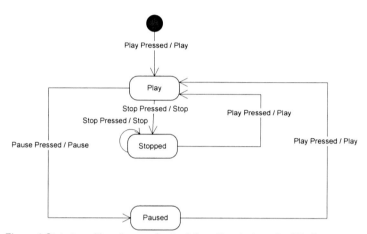

Figure 1 State transition diagram for the interaction design of a CD player

Window Navigation Diagrams

A window navigation diagram models the windows and the navigation paths between them. This model is a tool used to depict the sequence and variation of windows that can occur within a session (Whitten et al. 2001). Figure 2 illustrates the window navigation diagram of a simple application that allows a user to go from the main menu to a printing or save windows.

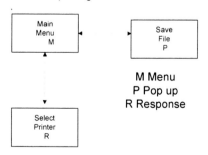

M Menu
P Pop up
R Response

Figure 2 Window Navigation Diagram

The WIMP interface

Graphical user interfaces (GUI) were introduced in 1984 by Apple when introducing the Macintosh. However, it is because Microsoft Windows is available on the popular IBM PC and compatible machines that the use of the GUI has spread around the world to the point that this has become the standard for desktop computing.

The popularity of Windows resides on the fact that users don't need to type commands but instead use the mouse to click on icons and menus. The mouse is used in Windows by the user to launch programs and manipulate objects on the screen. These objects were categorized in four areas that together formed the acronym WIMP: window, icon, menu, and pointing device.

Window

Windows are areas of the screen that behave as if they were independent terminals and can contain text or graphics. They can be moved, resized or overlap. Windows can obscure each other, or can be laid out next to one another. Windows have scrollbars that allow the user to move the contents of the window up and down or from side to side and title bars that describe the name of the window

The WIMP interface standard includes a set behaviours that the designer needs to follow when building interfaces. In any Windows interface, the user can open a window in one of four ways (Buttow 2007):

- Click on an icon on the desktop that links to the program. If the icon is a document, the program that is associated with the document opens automatically.

- Double-click on an icon or link within a window.

- Click a menu option in a program. For example, click New from the File menu in Microsoft Word.

- Click on a button or icon in the taskbar or Dock.

Users can move more than one window open at one time and one window might keep information for different tasks. One way that GUIs keep different tasks within one window is the multiple-document interface, or MDI. MDI uses tabs to keep track of separate documents within a window. In one type of MDI interface, you can click on the tab to go directly to that document without moving to a different window.

One example of a tabbed MDI interface is Internet Explorer 7, which keeps different Web pages in different tabs. If the window only keeps information of one task in one document, this window can be classified as a single-document interface or SDI.

A window can also open a dialog box, which is a smaller window designed to have the user set settings and make decisions. One example of this window is found Microsoft Word when the user wants to print a document since a print dialog box appears for the user to determine what printer to use, how many copies to print and other different settings required to print the document.

Windows can be maximized so they fill the user's entire screen in order to increase the working space area or to get full attention of a particular task. The Maximize, Minimize, and Close buttons appear in the title bar. In Windows, these buttons are on the right side of the title bar.

Icon

Windows uses metaphors to represent information like a desktop where files are located in folders and programs and other information can be organized on the screen. These metaphors are small pictures or images that represent some object in the interface often a window or action and are known as icons. Icons can represent if windows can be closed down (iconised). Icons can have various highly stylized or realistic representations and normally represent many accessible windows and applications available to be launched. Few popular icons found in the Windows operating systems are shown in figure 3:

Figure 3 Popular Windows icons

Menu

The menu displays a set of choices of operations or services available on the application and requires option selected with a pointer. However, they require a lot of screen space but they might be set so they only appear when they needed. Pull-down menus display a menu bar at top of the screen while pop-up menus appear at a desired location. An example of a pull-down menu is shown in figure 4 below:

Figure 4 Pull-down menu

In order to save space, cascading menus can be used to organize the menu in a hierarchical structure where a menu selection opens a new menu and this might open another one and so on till the design structure is satisfied. In addition, keyboard accelerators can be used to use a key combination to have the same effect as menu items. These accelerators are usually the first letter of the menu item or Ctrl + a letter,

When designing menus, the interaction designer needs to deal with issues such as the type of menu to use, menu items, how to group items and choice of keyboard accelerators.

Pointer

Windows relies on the mouse, a hardware device used to move a pointer on the screen in order to perform an action such as dragging or selecting an object. Other pointers include joystick, trackball, cursor keys or keyboard shortcuts. Pointers can have a great variety of images in order to represent different states such as normal select, help select, running on the background, busy and precision select like the ones in figure 4.

Figure 4. Pointer images

Summary

Conceptual design was covered and several tools to support this design were introduced including brainstorming, card sort, personas, scenarios, semantic networks and cognitive walkthroughs.

Interaction design models were introduced as useful tools for analyzing and understanding interface design. The GOMS and Keyboard Level Model (KLM) predictive models were introduced as tools to describe interaction designs and predict interactions performance. In addition, the state transition and windows navigation diagrams were covered as tools to document interaction designs.

Windows, icons, menus and pointers interface components were covered and their behaviours and standards explained.

References

Ashley, G. 1997, *WIMP Interfaces* [online] [12th Dec 2007] Available from World Wide Web: <http://www-static.cc.gatech.edu/classes/cs6751_97_winter/Topics/dialog-wimp/>

Badre, A. 2003, *Shaping Web Usability: Interaction Design in Context*, Addison Wesley Professional.

Butow, E. 2007, *User Interface Design for Mere Mortals*, Addison Wesley Professional.

Card, S., Morn, T. P., and Newell, A. 1980, The keystroke-level model for user performance with interactive systems, *Communications of the ACM,* 23, pp.396-210.

Card, S., Moran, T. P., and Newell, A. 1983, *The Psychology of Human-Computer Interaction,* Lawrence Erlbaum Associates, Hillsdale, NJ .

Dix, A., Finlay., Abowd, G., & Beale, R. 1998, *Human-computer interaction,* Prentice Hall, Upper Saddle River, NJ.

Hackos, J. T., and Redish J. 1998, User and Task Analysis for Interface Design. John Wiley & Sons. New York.

Heim, S. 2007, *The resonant interface,* Addison-Wesley, Boston MA.

Hochstein L., 2002, GOMS [online] [12th Dec 2007] Available from World Wide Web: <http://www.cs.umd.edu/class/fall2002/cmsc838s/tichi/printer/goms.html>

John, B. and Kieras, E. 1996, The GOMS Family of User Interface Analysis Techniques: Comparison and Contrast, *ACM Transactions on Computer-Human Interaction, vol 3 no,4,* pp. 320-351.

Rees, M., White, A. & Bebo, W. 2001, *Designing Web Interfaces,* Prentice Hall.

Saffer, D. 2006, *Designing for Interaction: Creating Smart Applications and Clever Devices,* Peachpit Press.

Zhang, Z. 2008, Cognitive Walkthrough, [online] [12th Dec 2007] Available from World Wide Web: < http://www.usabilityhome.com/FramedLi.htm?CognWalk.htm>

Discussion questions

5. Choose a task that involves multiple people and provide a use case for the task. This may be something that is performed at work or in an academic department. It must be large enough to provide an opportunity to create the Use Case.

6. Discuss some of the ways users can be involved in the design process.

7. Compare and contrast the methods used for observation and elicitation. Discuss what they are best suited for, when they should be applied and what results can be expected.

8. Choose three typical computing tasks that you perform regularly. Provide a Task Decomposition for each task and then provide an HTA of these same tasks.

Activities

For this chapter, you are required to submit a document that defines the personas for the primary stakeholders

Your are also required to submit evidence of the at least three of the following activities
- Brainstorming – Submit evidence of the brainstorming sessions (this may include digital photos of any multimedia tools such as post-its tacked to a wall)

- Card Sort – Submit the cards (or a scan of the cards) and the results of the sorting sessions

- Scenarios – Submit a document that describes the scenarios

- Flowcharts – Submit the flowcharts in an electronic format (Visio, Word etc.)

- Cognitive Walkthroughs – Submit the results of the walkthroughs (this can be a list of problems that were discovered)

In addition, choose a particular aspect of your proposed design and create a GOMS and a KLM analysis. Include all of the possible methods of accomplishing the tasks involved in that aspect of the design.

Sample Solution Conceptual Design

A document that defines the personas for the primary stakeholders

Local school leavers: Khalid
- Attends state school in Hammad Town
- does not have a computer
- lives in moderate sized house with five brothers and sisters
- not much personal space
- accesses email internet at friends houses or internet cafes
- will judge the quality of a company or institution by the quality of the website
- wants information quickly

Current students: Zainab
- lives with parents and three sisters
- Has a portable Macintosh
- wishes to study Visual Design and work as a designer in the advertising sector
- has three different email accounts, all accessed on line
- avid FaceBook user

Descriptive personas
1. Dana is currently five hundred kilometres away, at another university studying business. Her father is Jordanian, her mother is German. She has tried several university programmes, including one in Paris, but did not like the teaching style and approach at any of them, including her current one. She is tired of changing

50

programmes and when she heard good reports of this university and it's more practical curriculum she decided to find out more.

She uses her lap top with Wi-Fi connection to access her email and to visit two sites in particular: YouTube and Face Book, on which she spends between three and four hours a day. She likes the way those sites are organised. She sometimes makes spelling mistakes in her search criteria but usually this doesn't stop her from finding what she wants. She plans to work in tourism-related business to gain experience before starting her own company. She will probably make her judgement about the university based on her session on the website, since she is unable to visit in person.

2. Yusuf is currently head of eServices for a large company. He has been approached by the university to take on some students as interns. He has heard good reports about the university and wants to find out a little more about the way the programmes are taught before agreeing to the request.

He has a Master of Science and has worked in the field of e-Communications project management for many years.

B) Evidence of the at least three of the following activities

Scenarios
Scenario 1: Download Enrolment form
A school leaver wishes to apply for enrolment at the university
The university requires the prospective student to present themselves physically to student services with a valid identity card and originals of school records for sighting by university staff. There is also a long form to complete which can take anything up to thirty minutes to do. The student would at least like to have the chance of filling out this form beforehand for two reasons:
- questions that require extra research, or unforeseen requests for copies of documents can be dealt with before hand, removing the need for return visits
- time that would be normally spent at the university queuing to request the form and filling it in would no longer be wasted

The student types the address in a search engine, and then clicks the link to the website.

The home page is fast loading and the words "apply to be a student" are indicated clearly toward the top of the screen.

A link is also provided in the search result if the prospective student should type and even misspell several keywords relating to enrolment procedures of applications.
The link leads to another page with a link to a printable version of the application document. The student prints it out and completes the form.
Scenario 2: Access the student intranet
A current student, Sarah, wishes to access the university intranet from an internet cafe and has forgotten the URL.
The student wants to upload an assignment before deadline in five minutes after which the upload function will be deactivated.

The student enters the URL for the public website and sees the clearly displayed link to the login page. The user enters the user ID and password then is directed to a list of programmes and course that only he or she is currently enrolled in. The upload assignment link is accessible with only one click and directs the file to turn it in.

Scenario 3: Apply for a job
A foreign teacher, George, has heard of the university's recruitment drive and wants to apply for a position at the university that should be advertised in the Vacancies section.

Flowchart
See attached Visio file

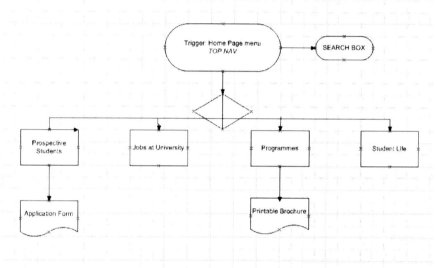

Cognitive Walkthrough
Scenario: Download Enrolment form
1. From the Home Page, click on "prospective students" link
2. From the "prospective students" Page click on "applications" link
3. Click on Download Enrolment form
4. Click on Open Document when PDF has arrived
5. Click on print icon or CTRL+P
6. Click OK to Print form

In the next version the form is presented in a sidebar on the home page
1. From the Home Page, click on "download student application form" link to be found in a side menu
2. Click on Open Document when PDF has arrived
3. Click on print icon or CTRL+P
4. Click OK to Print form

By putting one of the key reasons for visiting the site on the Home Page the user has achieved to goal in 4 steps and 4 clicks. The first method requires 6 steps and six clicks as it embeds the desired form link deep in the tree structure of the website, forcing the user to download many pages large image files.

Other common scenarios that could be developed include:
- Scenario 2: Access the student intranet
- Scenario 3: Apply for a job
- Scenario 4: watch a video about student life
- Scenario 5: Contact a programme manger
- Scenario 6: find information about a programme including a contact phone number for the programme manager

For maximum client-centred design to be achieved, it is recommended that quick links to these goals be clearly identifiable on the home page, probably in a side bar menu rather than in any drop down mouse- over triggered sub menus.

C) Choose a particular aspect of your proposed design and create a GOMS and a KLM analysis. Include all of the possible methods of accomplishing the tasks involved in that aspect of the design.

GOMS for printing a student enrolment form (from Home Page)
. [select GOAL: USE-SEARCH-METHOD

MOVE-CURSOR-TO-SEARCH-BOX

. CLICK-SEARCH-BOX

. TYPE-APPLY-FORM

. MOVE-CORSOR-TO-GO-BUTTON

. CLICK- GO-BUTTON]

. [select GOAL: USE-MENU-METHOD

MOVE-CURSOR-TO-PROSPECTIVE- STUDENTS -BUTTON

. CLICK- PROSPECTIVE-STUDENTS-BUTTON]

. MOVE-CURSOR-TO-DOWNLOAD-APPLICATION-FORM-LINK

. CLICK-LINK

. MOVE-CURSOR-TO-PRINT-ICON

. CLICK-ICON

. MOVE-CURSOR-TO-OK-BUTTON

. CLICK-BUTTON]

KLM for printing a student enrolment form (from Home Page)

a) Use menu method

Description	Operation	Time (sec)	
Reach for mouse	H[mouse]	0.40	
Move pointer to Pros. Students	P[menu item]		1.10
Click the Pros. Students	K[mouse]		0.20
Move pointer to Download link	P[menu item]		1.10
Click the link	K[mouse]	0.20	
Move pointer to print icon	P[menu item]	1.10	
Click the icon	K[mouse]	0.20	
Move pointer to OK button	P[menu item]	1.10	
Click the button	K[mouse]		0.20
TOTAL			**5.6**

b) Use search method

Description	Operation	Time (sec)	
Reach for mouse	H[mouse]	0.40	
Move pointer to Search box	P[menu item]	1.10	
Click the Search box	K[mouse]	0.20	
Home on keyboard	H[Keyboard]	0.40	
Specify word "apply"	M5K [mouse]	2.35	
Hit arrow or enter	K[keyboard]	0.20	
Reach for mouse	H[mouse]	0.40	
Move pointer to Download link	P[menu item]		1.10
Click the link	K[mouse]	0.20	
Move pointer to print icon	P[menu item]	1.10	
Click the icon	K[mouse]	0.20	
Move pointer to OK button	P[menu item]	1.10	
Click the button	K[mouse]		0.20
TOTAL			**8.95**

Chapter 5

Physical design and prototyping

In chapter 5, Physical design techniques and Interaction design guidelines principles are covered. Interaction design guidelines will be introduced.

Interaction Design Principles

There are many approaches to interaction design, since it can be very subjective, it is important to take into consideration basic interface design principles that don't tell you what you should build but provide guidance in terms of industry trends and basic characteristic that users look for when using interactions.

The reality is that is that there is no universal standard when it comes to interface design. However, it is important that the designers get familiar with different visions in order to make their own. In this lecture, several guiding principles that have been found to be useful are covered. The basic deign principles that drive most interaction guidelines are identified by Rees et al (2001) as follows:

- Consistency
- Simplicity
- Context

Consistency is a property that makes an interaction predictable from the user's perspective. To be classified as consistent, an interaction must conform to follow some to two basic rules. First, the interface must show consistency in the labels used for it. For example, the choice of menu labels and other words used to signify actions must have single meanings with no scope for ambiguity or never use two different words for the same task. The second rule is that all user actions must be reversible; in other words, everything must have an "undo" feature. Any exceptions must be clearly marked for the user with a warning dialog.

Simplicity can be achieved by following the following guidelines (Rees et al 2001):

- Show no more than is needed to achieve the desired user goal.
- Require a minimum of input from the user.
- Keep both the user and the task in focus.
- Make important concepts particularly clear.
- Use visual representations with direct manipulation (where possible).

The designer should ask if a new feature will make it easier for the user to achieve the primary goals, or if it is just unnecessary sophistication. For the user, the benefit of a simple interface is a clean design with visual refinement, no superfluous features, and clear, direct operations using familiar representations.

Clarity is important to achieve simplicity, this should be embedded at all levels of an interaction as indicated below (Rees et al. 2001):

- Information representation
- Organization and naming of interface controls

- Flow of control (dynamic behavior)
- Screen layout

Context refers to ability that the interaction should appear as a sequence of easily identifiable and distinct interface views. Contextual visibility can be incorporated into an interaction with three major tools (Rees et al. 2001):

1. What-you-see-is-what-you-get (WYSIWYG). This is technical slang for presenting information on the screen in the identical form (within display constraints) as it will appear in other media (such as paper and audio/visual). This includes both text and images—drawings, pictures, and (given the technology) moving images and sound.
2. Properties. Each visual object possesses a range of attributes (size, shape, color, and other parameters) that can be controlled by the user. This property information appears on the screen in property boxes.
3. Dialogs. Whenever small amounts of information (text, number, option, yes/no) must be solicited from the user, use a minor variation on the interface view known as a dialog box. This disappears when the input is achieved.

Although these three principles are useful in the design of any interaction, there are many other more sophisticated principles that have been developed by different researchers and industry. Three of these examples are found in Table 1 (Shneiderman),Table 2 (Mayhew), and Table 3 (IBM).

Consistency	All parts of interface use similar words, sequences of tasks, etc.
Shortcuts	Shortcuts are included for users who are familiar with the application
Useful Feedback	All user actions have some form of feedback
Group actions together	Group actions have a start, middle, and finish
Error Handling	Make the application robust so user cannot accidentally "kill" it and have simple methods of handling errors
Back out of actions	Allow users to undo tasks without penalty
User control	Give users control of the application rather than the application controlling the user
Short-term memory load	Keep displays simple with limited need for remembering

Table 1. Shneidernan's "Eight Golden Rules of Dialog Design" (Schneiderman, 1983)

User compatibility	Know your user – understand the concepts of cognition
Product compatibility	Keep the UI similar to other products so the user can immediately be productive
Task compatibility	The flow of the application matches the activity that which is being performed
Work flow compatibility	The application facilitates the transition

	between tasks to be completed
Consistency	All parts of interface uses similar words, sequences of tasks, etc.
Familiarity	The UI includes concepts and vocabulary that the user is already familiar with.
Simplicity	Make the interface simple
Direct manipulation	Users controls objects on a screen rather than using language to start some action
Control	UI should be set up to give the user the feeling of being in control – perhaps with a toolbox, etc.
WYSIWYG	Whatever the user sees on the screen is what is printed out in reports
Flexibility	Include various ways of doing things that accommodate the different level of skills
Responsiveness	All user actions have some form of feedback
Invisible technology	Hide the technology from the user and show only what they need to see to complete a task.
Robustness	Make the application robust so user cannot accidentally "kill" it
Protection	If users make mistakes, have simple methods of handling errors
Ease of learning and use	The application is easy to learn, but also is efficient for seasoned users

Table 2. Mayhew's "General Principles of User Interface Design" (Huang, 1997)

Simplicity	Keep UI simple and straightforward
Support	Provide user with a variety of ways to complete a task and allow them to divide the work into subtasks
Familiarity	Build on users' knowledge of previous applications
Obviousness	Make objects and how to work with them intuitive
Encouragement	Make actions predictable and reversible
Satisfaction	Create a feeling of progress and achievement
Accessibility	Users should be able to access any object that they need
Safety	Keep the user out of trouble – protect them when they make errors
Versatility	The UI should allow a variety of interaction techniques (menus, dialog boxes, shortcuts, etc)
Personalization	Allow users to customize that interface to improve their productivity
Affinity	The application should support the user model – a reasonable representation of the task to be completed

Table 3. IBM's "Design Principles for Tomorrow" (Huang, 1997)

Although there are many design principles in the industry and academia, they all have similarities in terms simplicity, consistency and context.

User Interface Design Guidelines

In the previous section, interface design principles were introduced. In practice, industry is mainly driven by interface design guidelines that were prepared with the design principles in mind. These sets of principles and guidelines are constructed by "experts" in the area of interface design and construction. There are a number of important guides available and few of the most important are covered in this lecture. The main sources of user interface design guidelines are the large software houses, the computer manufacturers, and respected authors in the HCI literature.

One of the earliest attempts to provide a set of guidelines is the work of Smith and Mosier (1986). They worked for the Mitre Corporation and compiled 944 guidelines. Many of the guidelines refer to character-based screens, but include many guidelines for the GUI. The guidelines can be split into six sections that are still valid today:

1. Data entry
2. Data display
3. Sequence control
4. User guidelines
5. Data transfer
6. Data protection

Another important guideline used in industry is the GNOME (Human Interface Guidelines (HIG) http://library.gnome.org/devel/hig-book/stable/). This document tells you how to create applications that look right, behave properly, and fit into the GNOME user interface as a whole. The document covers different aspects such as usability principles, desktop integration, windows, menus, toolbars, controls, feedback, visual design, icons, user input, language, checklists and credit.

The Apple Desktop interface developed for the Macintosh computer provides a consistent and familiar computer environment in which people can perform their many tasks. The Apple Desktop interface is based on the assumption that people are instinctively curious: They want to learn, and they learn best by active self-directed exploration of their environment.

Apple produced its design guidelines in a form for all designers to use. Table 4 shows an abbreviated summary. The complete guideline can be found at (http://developer.apple.com/documentation/UserExperience/Conceptual/OSXHIGuidelines/X HIGIntro/chapter_1_section_1.html).

Guideline	Comments
Metaphors from the real world	Use concrete metaphors and make them plain, so that users have a set of expectations to apply to computer environments. Whenever appropriate, use audio and visual effects that support the metaphors.

Guideline	Comments
Direct manipulation	Users want to feel that they are in charge of the computer's activities.
See-and-point (not remember-and-type)	Users select actions from alternatives presented on the screen. The general form of user actions is noun-then-verb, or "Hey, you—do this." Users rely on recognition, not recall; they should not have to remember anything the computer already knows. Most programmers have no trouble working with a command-line interface that requires memorization and Boolean logic. The average user is not a programmer.
Consistency	Effective applications are both consistent within themselves and consistent with one another.
WYSIWYG	There should be no secrets from the user, no abstract commands that only promise future results. There should be no significant difference between what the user sees on the screen and what eventually gets printed.
User control	The user, not the computer, initiates and controls all actions.
Feedback and dialog	Keep the user informed. Provide immediate feedback. User activities should be simple at any moment, though they may be complex taken together.
Forgiveness	Users make mistakes; forgive them. The user's actions are generally reversible—let users know about any that are not.
Perceived stability	Users feel comfortable in a computer environment that remains understandable and familiar rather than changing randomly.
Aesthetic integrity	Visually confusing or unattractive displays detract from the effectiveness of HCI. Different "things" look different on the screen. Users should be able to control the superficial appearance of their computer workplaces—to display their own style and individuality. Messes are acceptable only if the user makes them—applications aren't allowed this freedom.

Table 4. Summary of Apple User Interface Guidelines

Other popular design guidelines include Windows Vista User Guidelines (http://www.microsoft.com/whdc/Resources/windowsxp/default.mspx), Windows XP - Guidelines for Applications (http://msdn.microsoft.com/en-us/library/aa511258.aspx) and Osf/Motif Style Guideline (http://www.s-and-b.ru/syshlp/motif_guide/MotifStyleGuide/TOC.html).

Prototypes

Before the HCI is implemented and tested with users, it is a good idea to prototype the interaction in order to get feedback from potential users. A prototype is a good tool that helps to communicate your design idea to your potential users. In general, there are two types of prototypes: high-fidelity prototypes that look and behave just like the final HCI would and low-fidelity prototypes that can be a simple pencil or digital drawing of the HCI that shows how this would look but without any dynamic behaviour.

High-fidelity prototypes are fully interactive and feel like the final product. High-fidelity prototypes have the advantages that can be used for the final implementation of the HCI as they allow integration with source code and the designer can detect interaction problems that cannot be identified with static low-fidelity prototypes. However, they require sophisticated technical skills in graphics design and programming that might not be available at the design stage of the HCI.

High-fidelity prototypes might be developed with the help of user interface tool kits that are used to program interactive HCIs. Some of these include Windows Forms, The Apple XCode toolkit, or the GTK and QT multiplatform toolkits. Tool kits require significant programming skills and might be difficult to use for a rapid prototype, Visual Interface Builders are better suited for quick prototypes since they don't require complex programming skills, some examples of this type of tools are Visual Studio .Net and JBuilder. For Web based applications, there are specialized tools that can be used to product high-fidelity prototypes such as Dreamweaver and Flash, these tools contain all the web interface components required to create internet based HCIs.

A demo video of a high-fidelity tool for prototyping can be found at http://www.altia.com/products_photoproto.php. This tool works with Photoshop and allows the creation of interactive HCIs and integration at the programming level.

Low-fidelity prototypes are mockups of the HCI either on paper or in a graphics file. For example, a low fidelity prototype can show how different elements and different pages of a Web site will look. Mockups are static and lack of any interactivity with the user.

Low-fidelity prototypes include wireframes that are web site page layouts or software window layouts that show where text, graphics, links, buttons, and other elements will appear on the page. A wireframe page can include active links to other wireframe pages or windows, thus providing a more interactive idea of how the pages or windows will work together.

Low-fidelity prototyping provides substantial advantages. Low-fidelity prototype tests produce substantive user feedback early in the development process and don't require complex technical skills such as programming or graphic design (Snyder 2003).

During this module, you will be introduced to MockupScreens (http://www.mockupscreens.com/). This is a low-fidelity prototyping tool that can be used to produce Mockups of the HCI. The tool supports Windows and Web interaction prototypes and it can be linked to the scenarios that were created last week.

Summary

The basic deign principles: consistency, simplicity and context were covered as the main framework for more sophisticated interaction design propositions such as the Shneidernan's and Mayhew's design principles. Interface design guidelines were covered and some examples emphasized. Low and high fidelity prototypes were introduced and their differences highlighted.

References

Heim, S. 2007, *The resonant interface*, Addison-Wesley, Boston MA.

Huang, M. 1997, Design Principles. [online] [12th Dec 2007] Available from World Wide Web: <http://www.cc.gatech.edu/classes/cs6751_97_winter/Topics/design-princ/>

Rees, M., White, A. & Bebo, W. 2001, *Designing Web Interfaces*, Prentice Hall.

Schneiderman, B. 1983, Direct Manipulation: A Step Beyond Programming Languages. *IEEE Computer*, vol. 16 no. 8 pp. 57-69.

Smith, S. L., & Mosier, J. N. 1986, Guidelines for designing user interface software. Report ESD-TR-86-278.   Bedford,   MA: The   MITRE   Corporation.

Snyder, C. 2003, *Paper Prototyping*. Morgan Kaufmann Publishers, San Francisco, CA.

Discussion questions

1. The Framework for Design Principles is a directed model that focuses on the goal of Usefulness. Choose three digital information devices and describe the qualities that make them useful. Then identify the functionality that supports that goal. Finally describe how the Presentation Filter fosters the Usability goal.

2. Choose three design principles and discuss how they can be applied to support the goal of comprehensibility.

3. Some application or device interfaces have steep learning curves. Choose one interface that has a steep learning curve and discuss the reasons for the inherent complexity and/or difficulty. Describe some ways that might make the interface more learnable, refer to the appropriate design principles.

4. Look at the icons used in the toolbar of any business application. Using what you find as examples, discuss why the everyday environment is so important.

5. Why should we look outside of the immediate task for which we are designing a user interface?

6. Watch the demo of the high-fidelity prototyping tool PhotoProto (http://www.altia.com/products_photoproto.php). What are the advantages and disadvantages of using this tool compared with a low-fidelity tool such as MockupScreens?

7. Identify three existing Web formats that are used by sites from different domains, for instance news or entertainment. Collect screen captures of at least three examples of each unique format, create a wireframe of each format (You can use Mockupscreens) and write a report that describes each format and their relationship with the domain content. You may argue that these formats do support the domain-specific content and tasks or you may argue against the format. You may also discuss the pros and cons together.

Activities

For this chapter, you are required to submit a document that contains the low-fidelity prototypes for the scenarios that were defined in chapter 4. You can use a low fidelity prototype tool such as MockupScreens (http://mockupscreens.com/).

In addition, use the Apple guidelines summary in table 4 of the lecture and use it as a checklist against your human interaction design and evaluate it according to the checklist. Prepare a report with your findings.

Activities Sample Solution

1_Download_Enrolment_Form

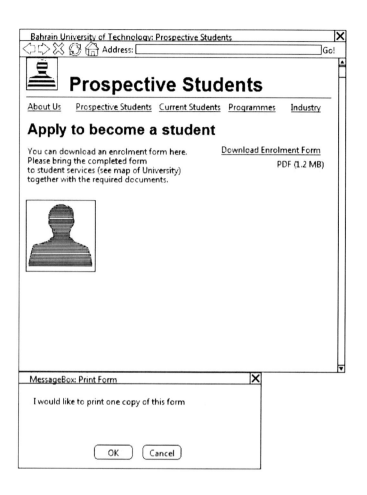

2_Access_student_Extranet

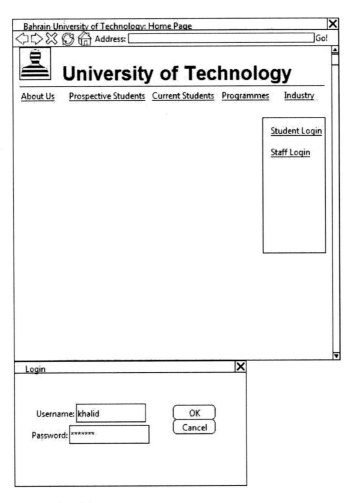

3_Apply_for_Job

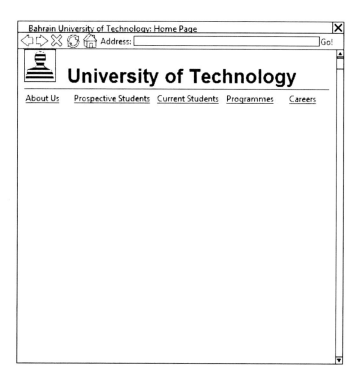

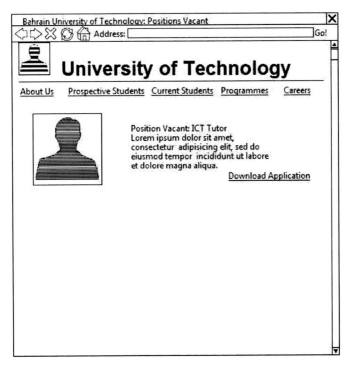

Apple Guidelines

Guideline	Comments
Metaphors from the real world	Use concrete metaphors and make them plain, so that users have a set of expectations to apply to computer environments. Whenever appropriate, use audio and visual effects that support the metaphors. *All three scenarios rely on clearly recognizable hypertext linking conventions (Blue underlining) and confirmation windows*
Direct manipulation	Users want to feel that they are in charge of the computer's activities. *All three scenarios rely on user initiation of searches though care is taken to reduce the navigation to a minimum of clicks*
See-and-point (not remember-and-type)	Users select actions from alternatives presented on the screen. The general form of user actions is noun-then-verb, or "Hey, you—do this." Users rely on recognition, not recall; they should not have to remember anything the computer already knows. Most programmers have no trouble working with a command-line interface that requires memorization and Boolean logic. The average user is not a programmer. *All three scenarios offer different sections for the variety of user requests. The simplicity of the navigation means the top level navigation is easily remembered as well as being clearly visible throughout any scenario on the website*
Consistency	Effective applications are both consistent within themselves and

Guideline	Comments
	consistent with one another. *All three scenarios employ linking with direct responses to user commands*
WYSIWYG	There should be no secrets from the user, no abstract commands that only promise future results. There should be no significant difference between what the user sees on the screen and what eventually gets printed. *Care is taken to make the PDF downloaded form as printer friendly as possible*
User control	The user, not the computer, initiates and controls all actions. *The successof clicking a link is indicated with the arrival of the new page or a "404 not found" error message in case of network failure*
Feedback and dialog	Keep the user informed. Provide immediate feedback. User activities should be simple at any moment, though they may be complex taken together. *All three scenarios use confirmation windows and rely on the client's printer interface for printing error messages or confirmation of success*
Forgiveness	Users make mistakes; forgive them. The user's actions are generally reversible—let users know about any that are not. *Not present in any of the three scenarios*
Perceived stability	Users feel comfortable in a computer environment that remains understandable and familiar rather than changing randomly. *All three scenarios maintain the same top navigation*
Aesthetic integrity	Visually confusing or unattractive displays detract from the effectiveness of HCI. Different "things" look different on the screen. Users should be able to control the superficial appearance of their computer workplaces—to display their own style and individuality. Messes are acceptable only if the user makes them—applications aren't allowed this freedom. *All three scenarios will consistently reflect a clean visual design – modern and uncluttered in look and feel, yet deploying recognizable Website conventions throughout.*

Chapter 6

Auditory interfaces and Haptics

In this chapter, we will learn the use of auditory interfaces and haptics. Voice interfaces, audio digital file formats, speech to text, voice recognition and the different haptics technologies will be included in this seminar.

Auditory Interface

An auditory interface is one that interacts with the user purely through sound. This typically means speech input from the user and speech output and non-speech output from the system. Non-speech output may include earcons (auditory icons, or sounds designed to communicate a specific meaning), background music, and environmental or other background sounds (Cohen et al., 2004).

Sound can be used to enhance interactions, especially when the user is occupied and unable to monitor the interaction when this constantly changes. However, sound also can become disturbing if not used carefully. Auditory interfaces present unique design challenges in that they depend on the ability to communicate with a user through transient, or non-persistent, messages. The user hears something, and then it is gone. The HCI must be designed to not overload the user and do not unduly challenge short-term memory or learning ability (Cohen et al., 2004).

Auditory interfaces offer an additional opportunity based on effective use of nonverbal audio. Earcons can be used to deliver information (e.g., a sound indicating "voice mail has arrived") without interrupting the flow of the application. Distinctive sounds can be used to landmark different parts of an application, thus making it easier to navigate. Additionally, nonverbal audio such as background music and natural sounds can create an auditory environment for the user, thereby creating a unique sound and feel associated with a particular business or message (Cohen et al., 2004).

In addition, auditory interfaces need to be designed to accommodate the hearing loss experienced by older adults. This can include control background noise, increase volume of important sounds, and incorporate supplementary visual cues (Charness and Bosman, 1990). In addition, high-frequency sounds (greater than 4,000 Hz) should be avoided and preference given to sounds with reverberation in the range of 1,000 Hz to 2,000 Hz.

Human factors guidelines for making speech more comprehensible to older listeners also exist: (1) Avoid the need for high-frequency detection and discrimination; (2) improve the discrimination of acoustic cues by maximizing their pitch, spectral, and location differences; (3) enhance signal-to-noise ratios through volume adjustment and by minimizing background noise and reverberation; and (4) foster accurate speech perception through the use of clear, reasonably paced, redundant, and context-rich messages (Kline and Scialfa, 1997; Tun and Wingfield, 1997).

Auditory interfaces rely heavily on audio files to reproduce sound for non-speech outputs. There are quite a few audio formats although the trend is to create formats that are smaller in size or of higher quality. Some worth mentioning are the AU format developed by Sun Microsystems that can be recorded in both mono and stereo sound and at a number of different sampling rates (this gives the option of different qualities), the AIFF (Audio Interchange File Format) that was developed by Apple Computer that can be recorded in both 8- and 16-bit sounds, mono and stereo, at a wide variety of different sampling rates, allowing for a range of different file sizes, the WAV (Windows Audio/Video), jointly developed by Microsoft and IBM that is capable of recording mono and stereo sound and offers multiple sampling rates, bit depths, and compression schemes and the MIDI (.midi, .mid) MIDI (Musical Instrument Digital Interface) that is a computer language that contain information on notes, tempos, instruments, and various other assorted pieces of musical data, which is then applied to an existing library of digitally recorded instrument samples. This last type of audio files (MIDI) is not recorded audio but computer instructions so files are exceedingly small in comparison to other audio formats.

Voice Interface

Voice interfaces are auditory interactions that have speech input normally given as voice command. These are popular with phones and used by many banks for customers to perform their transactions.

A voice user interface (VUI) is what a person interacts with when communicating with a spoken language application. The elements of a VUI include prompts, grammars, and dialog logic (also referred to as call flow). The prompts, or system messages, are all the recordings or synthesized speech played to the user during the dialog. Grammars define the possible things callers can say in response to each prompt. The system can understand only those words, sentences, or phrases that are included in the grammar (Cohen et al., 2004).

When designing a voice user interface, there is a need to define a set of potential conversations between a person and a machine that makes a spoken language system.

Figure 1 shows the basic architecture of a spoken language system. It consists of a series of processing modules designed to take speech input (the user's utterance), understand it, perform any necessary computations and transactions, and respond appropriately. Following the response, the system waits for the next utterance from the user and repeats the sequence until the call has ended (Cohen et al., 2004).

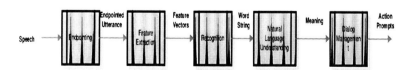

Figure 1 The architecture of a spoken language understanding system (Cohen et al., 2004).

The model first step is the endpointing that detects the beginning and end of speech. The system listens for the caller's input. The endpointer determines when the waveform, representing the vibrations of the caller's spoken utterance, has begun and then listens for a sufficiently long silence to indicate that the caller has finished speaking. The waveform is packaged and sent to the next processing module, which performs feature extraction. The feature extraction module transforms the endpointed utterance into a sequence of feature vectors that are lists of numbers representing measurable characteristics of the speech that are useful for recognition. The numbers typically represent characteristics of the speech related to the amount of energy at various frequencies. The recognition module uses the sequence of feature vectors to determine the words that were spoken by the caller. Following recognition, the natural language understanding module assigns a meaning to the words that were spoken. After the meaning of the caller's input has been determined, the dialog manager determines what the system does next such as accessing a database, play back information to the caller, perform a transaction, or play a prompt requesting more information from the caller (Cohen et al., 2004). Jurafsky and Martin (2000) provided a generic dialog management module that can be configured for a particular application.

Auditory interfaces might also benefit from text-to-speech synthesis and speaker verification technologies.

Text-to-Speech Synthesis

Text-to-speech (TTS) technology synthesizes speech from text. Auditory interfaces typically use recorded human speech to play prompts and messages to callers. However, certain applications, such as e-mail readers and news readers, have very dynamic data to which callers wish to listen. In those cases, given that the text of the messages cannot be predicted, you can use TTS technology to create the output speech (Cohen et al., 2004).

Although one the main problems with TTS is how much the synthesized speech sounds like real human speech (Naturalness), there have been tremendous advances in the naturalness of synthesized speech, largely because of the refinement of an approach called concatenative synthesis. A concatenative synthesizer uses a large database of segments of recorded speech. The output signal is created by concatenating a sequence of these prerecorded segments (Cohen et al., 2004).

Other issues with TTS are how well the listener can understand what is said, the correctness of what is synthesized and how well users tolerate extended listening without fatigue (Cohen et al., 2004).

Speaker Verification

Speaker verification technology is used for authentication. In some applications, speaker verification has been used to replace personal identification numbers (PINs) or to provide secure access to account and credit card information. This type of systems require the collection of a small amount of the caller's speech, which is used to build a model of the person's voice (voiceprint) so the user's voice can be compared to both the stored model and an imposter model (a model created from a combination of other speakers). A decision to accept or reject the caller is made based on how well the input speech matches each of those models (Reynolds and Heck 2001).

Haptics

Originated from the Greek "haptesthai and is the study and implementation of techniques and psychological effects of the physical interface is called haptics. Haptics in particular is related to the perception and manipulation of objects using the senses of touch and perception. Most of the haptic devices use two modes of sensation such as hearing and touch. Haptic interaction is symmetric and bidirectional. Haptic interfaces use inputs that detect touch or movement such as force sensitive resistors, thermistors, and capacitance sensors. Haptic devices communicate to the outside works by using devices that allow you to generate sensations of vibration and temperature. Some haptics technologies are discussed below.

Tactile Technologies

Tactile information is produced by perturbing the skin or by using input sensitive devices. The force-sensitive resistor (FSR) is one of the best sensors in the physical computing tool kit. FSRs convert mechanical force into electrical resistance. FSRs are typically designed to sense small amounts of force, such as the force of your finger pressing a button or keypad. The force of your body weight will quickly bring these sensors to their peak reading. Parallax (http://www.parallax.com), Images SI (http://www.imagesco.com), and Interlink Electronics sells carry a variety of FSR forms.

Flex sensors, look and work much like FSRs, but they vary resistance based on how much you bend them instead of how much you press on them. A good application is for sensing things that bend like fingers and hinges. They show up in a number of different virtual reality control gloves. You can find flex sensors at Infusion Systems (http://infusionsystems.com), Jameco (http://www.jameco.com), and Images SI.

For sensing the very lightest touch, a good possibility is capacitance sensors. The human body is something of a capacitor, always storing a small electric charge. Some capacitance sensors can detect human body's charge from distances of up to a meter and are used to measure analog distance. This is the technique used by the Theremin musical instrument (http://www.thereminworld.com).

Piezoelectric sensors are often used to detect strain or very slight force changes. These sensors produce a varying voltage when they are bent. They respond very quickly, and to slight changes. This type of devices is available from Digi-Key (http://www.digikey.com).

A byproduct of human touch is heat. You can determine if a user is touching an object by detecting an increase in heat using a thermistor. Thermistors convert heat into electrical resistance. Thermistors can be bought from http://www.maxim-ic.com.

Tactile information can be input also by perturbing the skin. Attaching electrodes to the user skin and reading involuntary responses like heart rate, skin reactions, and brain wave activity can be used to interact with the user. Galvanic skin response is one measurable quantity generated involuntarily by the body. It's well known as the basis for the polygraph, or lie detector. The theory behind is that a user sweats more when stressed, and that telling a lie is stressful.

The brain and muscles generate small electrical signals that can be picked up by electrodes strapped to your body. There are a few manufacturers of brainwave (electroencephalograph, or EEG) sensors and muscle movement (EMG) sensors. Infusion Systems makes an electromyograph, or EMG sensor, the Curl, for use with their controller box. IBVA

Technologies (http://www.ibva.com) makes an EEG and EMG sensor that interfaces with a Macintosh or PC. Brain Actuated Technologies (http://www.brainfingers.com) makes a similar system.

Tactile technologies are found in interactions for in simulators to more accurately project what happens in the real world. For example, flight simulators use tactile interfaces to tell the user what's happening. When a pilot in a simulation encounters a situation on the screen, the control stick will provide the same amount of resistance that the pilot would experience in that situation.

Touch screens

Touch screens are very popular haptic devices and are available from many suppliers. There are many commercial touch screens that are integrated into ordinary monitors. In addition to the usual video connection these will have a serial or USB connection for the touch information. Many of these devices work by getting the touch location by simply reading the mouse coordinates. You can also buy screens that can be attached to conventional monitors. Elo TouchSystems (http://www.elotouch.com) makes a number of both integrated touch screen monitors and add-on touch screens. The disadvantage of touch screens is that they generally will only read contact at one point at a time. This means that if you put all five fingertips on the screen, you won't get five discrete locations. Instead, the screen will report several different locations in succession in an inconsistent order.

There are some commercial multi touch pads but mainly used to build musical devices interfaces. This type of devices is becoming popular in places such as grocery stores, and ATM machines, cars that have a touch screen for accessing maps, radio stations and kiosks that provide services such as public Internet access or express check-in at airports. Touch interfaces are also widely used with mobile devices such as Personal Digital Assistants (PDAs) and Pocket PCs.

Force Feedback Displays

Haptic feedback devices can resist the force of your muscles, usually requires more power and more mechanical expertise than previous covered haptic devices. At the extremes of this are the mechanical systems used in simulators for training astronauts and for amusement park rides. Feedback displays mostly resembles a small robot arm and provide a point of interaction between a user and a virtual environment .

In feedback devices, kinaesthetic information is produced by exerting mechanical forces. Feedback devices are available for home use in the form force-feedback joysticks like the Sony Playstation DUALSHOCK, NINTENDO 64 Rumble Pack and Microsoft force feedback joystick. These devices are mainly geared towards a gaming market but also include a "haptic desktop"

Several high end devices exist such as the PHANToM. A Phantom device is a robot arm that is attached to a computer and used as a pointer in three dimensions, like a mouse is used as a pointer in two dimensions. SensAble Technologies manufactures several models of the Phantom (http://www.sensable.com/).

Telephone interfaces

Telephone user interfaces require you to use the telephone touch pad to interact with the program in the system. This is commonly used for such purposes as selecting the correct extension or department number when you call a company as well as accessing your answering machine voice mail system that your telephone company manages.

Summary

The auditory interaction was defined and the main characteristics covered. The voice interface model was covered and explained and the speech-to-text and speech verifications technologies mentioned as some examples of voice interface technologies. Haptic technologies were explained and its relevancy to HCI emphasized.
References

Heim, S. 2007, *The resonant interface,* Addison-Wesley, Boston MA.

Cohen M. H., Giangola J.P and Balogh J. 2004, *Voice User Interface Design,*: Addison Wesley Professional, Boston MA.

Charness, N. , and Bosman, E. A. 1990. Human factors and design for older adults. In J. E. Birren and K. W. Schaie (eds.), Handbook of the Psychology of Aging, Third Edition. San Diego: Academic Press.

Jurafsky, D., and J. Martin . 2000. *Speech and language processing: An introduction to natural language processing, computational linguistics, and speech recognition.* Upper Saddle River, NJ: Prentice Hall.

Kline, D. W. , and Scialfa, C. T. 1997. Sensory and perceptual functioning: Basic research and human factors implications. In A. D. Fisk and W. A. Rogers (eds.), Handbook of Human Factors and the Older Adult. San Diego, CA: Academic Press.

Reynolds, D., and L. Heck . 2001. Speaker verification: From research to reality. International Conference on Acoustics, Speech, and Signal Processing. Tutorial. Salt Lake City, Utah.

Tun, P. A. , and Wingfield, A. 1997. Language and communication: Fundamentals of speech communication and language processing in old age. In A. D. Fisk and W. A. Rogers (eds.), Handbook of Human Factors and the Older Adult. San Diego, CA: Academic Press.

Discussion questions

1. Speech Applications –Describe how Speech Applications function and the applications for which they are used. Include a discussion of the various file formats and their capabilities.
2. Redundant Coding – Describe occasions when auditory feedback is:
   a. Necessary, because other forms of feedback are either inappropriate or not possible, and how it can be presented
   b. Inappropriate due to particular external circumstance

3. Describe the differences between digital audio and MIDI files

4. Choose a particular domain and write a paper that describes how haptic interaction can be used to benefit the tasks involved in that domain. You can choose a domain from the following list or choose a different one that is not on the list.
   a. Teleoperation
   b. Medical
   c. Disabled
   d. Aerospace
   e. Scientific Visualizations
   f. Modeling
   g. Art
   h. Collaboration
   i. Data Representations – Graphs
   j. Gaming

Activities

For this chapter, you are required to submit a document that describes the use of sound and haptics in your proposed HCI design. Discuss the reasons for the application of auditory feedback and any other redundant coding that is involved in the relevant functionality. In addition, include the rational for using haptic interaction and a description of the physical components of the proposed design.

Activities sample solution

The use of haptics and sound is not part of the essential website interaction for most users, who will typically be adults aged between 17 and 50 with no significant impairment to their hearing or vision. Sound effects for standard web interaction are controlled by the user's browser version and settings and are not part of the coding. The website, however, will be developed in such a way that all content is adaptable to specialised or atypical browser environments.

Atypical browsing compatibility

The layer of sound and haptics will enter the design according to the following criteria:
World Wide Web Consortium guidelines on accessibility requires that coding for all web pages be prepared for specially adapted web browsers for those user with hearing or seeing impairments. Such browsers, sometimes called screen readers, are specially equipped browsers that take the text of a website and read it out using a computer based speech

synthesis application. The website must be tested in both normal browsers and screen reader (or audible) browsers. However, adherence to accessibility guidelines is the surest way of preparing content for current and future audio or haptic browsing.
The W3C accessibility guidelines include:

- making sure that image elements have the ALT attribute contains concise yet meaningful descriptions

- Making sure that the ALT attribute is not used on meaningless formatting elements like GIF bullets. (a descriptive alt tag will force screen readers to waste time on such useless text as "Bullet for link to home page" when only the link itself should be read out)

- ensuring that ALT attributes contain clear instructions as to the result of clicking on an image e.g. ALT="Click on this banner to return to home page"

- Captions and transcripts of audio elements

- Using clearer link names

- Text equivalence will be applied (van Duyne 2007), that is, making as much web content (images, audio and movie clips) accompanied with plain text, the most accessible media element on websites.

- audio descriptions of all multimedia and visual elements

- Preparing the accessibility elements for future modification. This is necessary since:

i) The W3C's accessibility guidelines are still a work in progress, and the website should be adaptable to new innovations.
ii) Accessibility facets of HTML5 are developed and integrated into major browsers for both desktop, public and mobile access

- Visually expressed data (graphs, table data instructions) must be accompanied by audio files containing the same information. This is especially so for content that is formatted in such a way that it may not be expressed coherently by a screen reader

- Avoid meaningless link names like "Click here". All links should be long enough to represent an accurate description of the target behind each link. Especially import for coherence in screen reader software.

- If the site uses a browser, reduce the amount of redundant text in the description of each result. Allow the user to tab quickly through the results by making the result content apparent in the first few words. E.g. Instead of:

"Updated minutes and abstract of the 2nd convention on international users of guidelines for web accessibility"

the text should put the main subject at the beginning:

"Web accessibility guideline: minutes and abstract of second convention etc"

If the user is not interested in the topic then the first three words will be enough and he or she can continue tabbing through the results list. This way of writing is a good tip for reading on screen as much as for audible browsers, since the eye gets as tired of redundant language as the ear.

In any consideration of the use of sound, it is important to note that
> *One of the most important considerations in designing audio for a non-visual interface is that the auditory space overloads much faster than the visual space. Initial user testing has highlighted the fact that too many sounds presented simultaneously will confuse the user. Short auditory clips are preferable to convey simple information quickly. Continuous sounds should be used sparingly and a hierarchy of significance of each sound should be determined before it is used.* (Yu 2005)

Showcase Kiosks

A version of the site will be available on kiosks at three strategically placed locations at the university (general reception x 1, student services x 2). The kiosks will contain 19 inch tactile screen. The casing will feature the university's recognisable brand, logo and colour schemes. The browser chosen will be the one with the most advanced haptic-enabled interface.
Authored in Virtual Reality Modelling Language (VRML) and requiring a haptic plug-in, the 3D interface is both an information tool and a way of promoting the cutting edge aspects of the university to first time visitors. There will be one kiosk at student services reception are that is both adjust in height to users in wheelchairs and equipped with a Braille keyboard.
Additional media will include short promotional and informative video clips on a range of subjects relating to enrolment, student life, university activities and degree programmes. These clips will contain an option for adding subtitles to the presentation.
Success and error signals will be accompanied by recognisable green (tick) and red (cross) icons, but sound will be avoided as a consideration to people within earshot.
It should be born in mind that an excess of sound can have negative results on the user experience and is often the source of complaints from users. Prospective students at the kiosk do not wish to have their browsing activities made known to people within earshot. Any sound layer must be accompanied by a clearly indicated mechanism for disabling (or enabling) the sound effects.
Since websites have visually rich GUI's, it is anticipated that the amount of adaptive development work will be larger for the visually impaired than for the hearing impaired.
There will be no attempt to integrate more sophisticated haptic interaction into the website at this point, largely due to the expense of implementing this newly-nascent technology. Use of exoskeletons, manipulator arms and vibrotactile systems were not deemed sufficiently appropriate for a public information website where funds could be better spent on improving general accessibility and providing richer multimedia content. For users who could benefit from such technology, namely those users with major disabilities, it was considered more cost effective to have volunteered staff available on rotation to provide direct assistance in any aspect of the information sharing or enrolment process
Given that the majority of users are between 17 and 20 and that the games culture has widespread popularity, it is proposed that there be a kiosk at student services equipped with a haptic mouse and a games style interface. The kiosk will be equipped with headphones to reduce irritation to bystanders of the rich audio content.
Users can navigate haptically through a 3D interface (using Immersive touch and other state of the art augmented reality applications), play educational games that record a high score to

be displayed on the scoreboard for all subsequent users to see, offer competitions and prizes. This strategy has several advantages:

1) Distinguishes the university as a technology leader and experimenter. Prospective students are made to feel that the university has a point of difference not shared by competing institutions

2) Provides incentives similar to customer loyalties techniques used in commercial and marketing contexts

3) Provides useful distraction for those forced to wait for scheduled interviews or while forms are processed

4) Showcase the work of current students from appropriate programmes (art work by visual design students, games designed by multimedia students, software from IT students etc)

Small screen compatibility

New mobile devices are equipped with touch screen and some are even applying haptic technology in the browser interface. This, again, is just one of the many devices that will display the content, not something that is controllable by the project developers. Examples of such mobile browsers include Android and Windows 7 devices where simulated button release/press sensation is sent to the fingers (Angel 2010)

References

Angel, J. (2010) *Haptic technology targets Android tablets* [Online] Available from: http://www.linuxfordevices.com/c/a/News/Immersion-TouchSense-2500/ (Accessed 16 November 2010)

van Duyne D. (2007) *The Design of Sites*, Prentice Hall

O'Malley, M & Hughes, S. (2003) *Simplified Authoring of 3D Haptic Content for the World Wide Web*, Mechanical Engineering and Materials Science, Rice University [Online] Available from: http://mahilab.rice.edu/sites/default/files/publications/161-getPDF.pdf (Accessed 16 November 2010)

Yu, W. Et. Al (2005) *Improving Web Accessibility Using Content-Aware Plug-ins* [Online] Available from: http://www.sarc.qub.ac.uk/~emurphy/papers/chi2005.pdf (Accessed 16 November 2010)

Chapter 7

Evaluation methods for HCI and Web Accessibility

In this chapter, Heuristic evaluation of interfaces is introduced. Methods for Conducting Usability Studies are included.

Evaluation of Usability

In this lecture we will introduce some common methods for evaluating interactions. The purpose of usability measurement determines which measures are appropriate and when they need to occur.

According to Chandler and Hyatt (2002), there are different approaches to evaluating usability and they fall into three main categories which are:

- Inspection methods
- Lab testing methods
- Surveys and customer reporting methods

Inspection methods do not involve customers. Members of the design team, product category experts, quality and productivity and/or human factors engineers apply a formal review process of the interaction to evaluate usability. These methods are usually quick and inexpensive to use. They also provide qualitative data used to derive some quantitative metrics. Because customers are not involved, however, it does not directly measure usability.

A few key inspection methods include heuristic evaluations and walk-throughs. Heuristic evaluations review an interaction against an established set of common usability principles. The review is based on the expertise of the reviewers. Walk-throughs simulate a customer's experience with the interaction. The results of the simulation are compared with the goals, expectations, and knowledge that a first-time customer is expected to have with an online store.

Another inspection method is the navigation stress test developed by Instone (2007) that is used for web interaction evaluation. The stress test method is simple and consists in 6 steps (Instone 2007):

1. Pick a page or pages randomly from deep within the site. Don't use the home page.
2. Print the page or pages in black and white. Remove the URL from the printed page.
3. Assume that you are a first-time visitor to the site and have arrived from a search engine results list. Alternatively, you could ask someone else who has never seen the site before to participate in the test, such as someone in your office or even a friend or family member.
4. Mark up the printed page with the symbols for each stress test question (See link http://instone.org/navstress for a complete set of stress questions). You may also add or delete from this list, depending on the type of site or user needs.
5. For questions that can't be answered, determine the cause. Is this a problem with this page only or with the navigation system as a whole?
6. Draw up recommendations for improving the navigation based on your findings.

The lab testing method involves the testing of representative users. Objective data is collected on customers' actual responses. This method can be diagnostic or evaluative.

This method normally consists in usability tests that are often structured as laboratory-based trials in which test users perform tasks that represent the way they might interact with the HCI.

The number of people tested is a key cost-driver and is highly debated in usability circles. Some feel that several, iterative tests with only a few people is better than a single test with twelve or more. Others feel that, in order to identify all problems, a larger sample size is needed.

Usability tests require planning. Kalbach (2007) suggests the following steps for usability testing:

1. Identify and recruit appropriate test participants. Create a test plan and protocol.
2. Set up a laboratory for observation and data collection.
3. Conduct the test. Analyze findings.
4. Present final recommendations.

The third type of method is to survey customers about their experiences on the usability of interactions. This method provides subjective data and is based on expressed feelings, attitudes, and perceptions of the interaction's usability and overall desirable qualities.

In this lecture the heuristic method will be covered in detail. This method is used for this module since it is inexpensive and can be easily conducted in few days. The usability testing method will be covered in week 8 since it is complex and requires a full week to understand it better.

Heuristic Evaluation

Heuristic evaluations are based on the expertise of a set of reviewers. The evaluator makes judgments as to the compliance with recognized principles, or heuristics. Heuristics generally apply across situations and are used to predict potential problems with the interaction.

Heuristic evaluation has the advantage of being easy to use and does not require expensive lab settings. The idea is to have a reviewer in the shoes of a user and perform the evaluation with the heuristic principles in mind. The idea of this method is to have a set of evaluators (from 3 to 5) check from compliance with usability principles ("heuristics"). These evaluations can be performed on a physical prototype or actual interaction implementation.

Nielsen (1994) identified some potential problems that can be detected with heuristic evaluations based on a rank of severity (0-5):

0   No problem at all
1. Cosmetic issues only
2. Minor problems present for some users
3. Major problems are present; important to fix
4. Catastrophe and unusable for nearly all users; imperative to fix

For example, let's say that the interface used the string "save" on the first screen for saving the user's file, but used the string "write file" on the second screen. Since users might be confused by this different terminology for the same function this can be considered a problem of rank 3.

Kalbach (2007) identifies 3 steps for heuristic evaluation:

1. Prepare: Agree on who will do the review. At this step, it is important to determine the principles for evaluation. Standard heuristics are available, but consider expanding them and include specific ones to the type of interaction that is under evaluation. It is important to have stakeholders approve your evaluation process.
2. Execute: Go through the interaction prototype, focusing on one principle at a time. For each heuristic, provide a severity rating from 0 to 4 according to Nielsen's ranking.
3. Consolidate: Discuss your findings with other reviewers. Agree on the potential problem areas and on the interpretation of issues. Look for patterns across your notes and between reviewers, summarize these and determine appropriate recommendations for addressing the identified issues. At the end of this step is important to create a presentation for the project team and stakeholders. Develop a plan for addressing the identified issues.

Nielsen (1994) proposed 10 general "heuristics" that can be used in heuristic evaluations. These are:

- **Visibility of system status**: The system should always keep users informed about what is going on, through appropriate feedback within reasonable time. This means that is important to pay attention to response time, if the user is waiting for responses from the system for more than one second, it is necessary to include a visual aid that indicates the progress of a specific activity.

- **Match between system and the real world**: The system should speak the users' language, with words, phrases and concepts familiar to the user, rather than system-oriented terms. Follow real-world conventions, making information appear in a natural and logical order. This means that the interaction should not use any technical jargon and keep the interaction in simple terms that can be understood by the user.

- **User control and freedom**: Users often choose system functions by mistake and will need a clearly marked "emergency exit" to leave the unwanted state without having to go through an extended dialogue. Support undo and redo. This means that the interaction should not force down fixed paths. This heuristic is often accomplished by using wizards that require the user to click "next" before going to the next step but always with an option to cancel in case a mistake has been made.

- **Consistency and standards**: Users should not have to wonder whether different words, situations, or actions mean the same thing. Follow platform conventions.

- **Error prevention**: Even better than good error messages is a careful design which prevents a problem from occurring in the first place. Either eliminate error-prone conditions or check for them and present users with a confirmation option before they commit to the action. This means to make objects, actions, options and directions visible or easily retrievable.

- **Recognition rather than recall**: Minimize the user's memory load by making objects, actions, and options visible. The user should not have to remember information from one part of the dialogue to another. Instructions for use of the system should be visible or easily retrievable whenever appropriate.

- **Flexibility and efficiency of use**: Accelerators -- unseen by the novice user -- may often speed up the interaction for the expert user such that the system can cater to both inexperienced and experienced users. Allow users to tailor frequent actions. This is normally accomplished with the use of shortcuts and hot keys that can be used to easy the interaction to expert users.

- **Aesthetic and minimalist design**: Dialogues should not contain information which is irrelevant or rarely needed. Every extra unit of information in a dialogue competes with the relevant units of information and diminishes their relative visibility.

- **Help users recognize, diagnose, and recover from errors**: Error messages should be expressed in plain language (no codes), precisely indicate the problem, and constructively suggest a solution. Good error messages should indicate that something has gone wrong, be in a human-readable language, be polite and not blame the users, describe the problem, give constructive advice on how to fix the problem. Error messages should be visible and preserve as much as the user's work as possible. If possible, try to guess the correct action and let the users pick a possible fix from a list. It is also advisable to provide a link to pages with an explanation to the problem.

- **Help and documentation**: Even though it is better if the system can be used without documentation, it may be necessary to provide help and documentation. Any such information should be easy to search, focused on the user's task, list concrete steps to be carried out, and not be too large.

In addition to the heuristics of Nielsen, Kalbach (2007) proposed the following heuristics specific to web based interactions:

- **Balance**: The number of navigation options presented is balanced with the depth of the site's structure.
- **Ease of Learning**: Using navigation is intuitive and easily learned.
- **Efficiency**: Findings and using navigation options is easy. Paths to information are short.
- **Consistency**: The presentation and interaction of navigation options is consistent and predictable. Inconsistency is appropriately used to show contrast and priority.

- **Clear Labels**: Navigation labels are unambiguous and predictable. Categories are meaningful and mutually exclusive.
- **Orientation**: It is clear where you are within the site on each page.
- **Exploration**: The navigation promotes free exploration and information discovery.
- **Differentiation**: The site facilitates scanning and browsing. It also allows people to quickly differentiate relevant information from non-relevant information.
- **Information Use**: After finding relevant information, people can use it appropriately. They can capture content for integration into personal information sources.
- **Modes of Searching**: The navigation supports multiple modes of seeking (known-item, exploration, don't-know-what-you-need-to-know, re-finding) that are appropriate to the site.

Heuristic evaluation is very fast compared with other evaluation techniques since each evaluator can produce a report in a matter of hours. It does not require user participants so this minimizes the complexity for the evaluation. However, the question is how many evaluators shall we use for an evaluation? Nielsen (1994) in a study, found that one evaluator generates poor results since it only finds 35% of usability problems while 5 evaluators find 75% of the usability problems. Although the more reviewers you have in a study the closest you get to 100% of the usability problems, according to Nielsen it is more cost effective to have between 3 to 5 reviewers for an evaluation.

Heuristic evaluation can be also accelerated with the use of checklists. Instead of overarching principles, concrete test statements are the basis for the review. Your responses to each statement may be yes or no, or you could use a severity scale. A sample checklist can be found at http://www.stcsig.org/usability/topics/articles/he-checklist.html.

Given the high cost of conducting interaction evaluations, a new trend is towards automated evaluation. Consider one of the several programs and services that run automated accessibility checks across a web site. These tools crawl through your code and compare it to known standards guidelines and then highlight potential problems. For example, if all images don't have alt attributes, the software will flag it. Free tools include Wave (http://wave.webaim.org), InFocus (www.ssbtechnologies.com/products/infocus) and AccVerify (www.hisoftware.com/access/newvIndex.html).

Web Accessibility

Web accessibility is about building web sites, applications, and pages that present few barriers to use as possible for anyone, regardless of ability and the device used to access the information. Web accessibility should accommodate persons with disabilities and also provide access to those using slower connections that normally have the images tuned off as well as increase interoperability with mobile devices such as PDAs, cell phones and Black berries.

People's disabilities that can impact the Web can be placed in four major groups according to Navarro (2000):

- **Visual Disabilities:** Users might be fully or partially blind, have impaired color vision, or simply need the use of corrective lenses. Graphics that aren't labeled or described, a lack of keyboard-based navigation support, or even small print and low-contrast colors can result in barriers to information.
- **Hearing Disabilities:** A lack of captioning, transcripts, or other alternative distributions of audio-based content can leave hearing-impaired users without important information.
- **Physical Disabilities:** Some users might have limited skill or dexterity for typing, operating a mouse or trackball, or other selection pointer.
- **Cognitive and Neurological Disabilities:** A lack of clear and consistent labeling, navigation systems, and other visual cues can confuse many users. Excessive use of jargon on sites that will be accessed by the lay-public, or highly technical information presented to such an audience without illustration, can inhibit comprehension. Additionally, flashing, flickering, or other high-frequency movements can have serious consequences for users dealing with epilepsy or other light- and motion-sensitive conditions.

In 1997 the World Wide Web Consortium began research into what is now termed "universal accessibility" on the Web or W3C Accessibility initiative (WAI). The WAI program has five primary goals:

- Ensure that new Web technologies support accessibility.
- Develop guidelines for implementing accessibility features.
- Develop tools to evaluate and facilitate accessibility.
- Publish materials and conduct events that educate the public and Web-development community about accessibility, and perform other outreach tasks.
- Coordinate with research and development, reviewing adoption rates of accessible techniques, collaborating with outside research projects, and doing other tasks as required.

The most relevant document created by the WAI for HCI designers is the Web Content Accessibility guidelines. The first design guidelines document released was the WCAG 1.0

These guidelines have several related checkpoints organized according to three different priority levels from Priority 1 (most critical for web accessibility) to Priority 3 (important but having less impact on overall accessibility). At www.w3.org/TR/1999/WAI-WEBCONTENT-19990505, each of the checkpoints are listed following their related guidelines along with their priority level. For a view of the checkpoints organized according to their priority level, go to www.w3.org/TR/WCAG10/full-checklist.html.

The WCAG 1.0 document contains 14 guidelines that can be summarized as:

- Guideline 10: Use interim solutions. This guideline requires the designer to ensure that the recommended guideline is still valid and useful and has not become obsolete due to new technologies.

- Guideline 11: Use W3C technologies and guidelines. The W3C specifications were designed with accessibility features built into them. So, following these specifications should result in greater accessibility for all.
- Guideline 12: Provide context and orientation information. This guideline encompasses using titles for frames to ensure that the purpose of each frame is clearly stated, to use elements, such as optgroup, within a select form control to group related options together, to use fieldset to group related form controls together, to describe the fieldset contents with a legend, and to explicitly associate form controls with their labels.
- Guideline 13: Provide clear navigation mechanisms. Clearly marked navigation menus that are consistent across a site can be enhanced by using a site map, providing metadata by using link relationships and other information about the author, date of publication, and the type of content they contain.
- Guideline 14: Ensure documents are clear and simple. This guideline is designed to help everyone by making documents more readable and more readily understood.

WCAG 2.0 will be completed in 2008 and is W3C candidate recommendation. WCAG 2.0 revolves around four basic principles for web accessibility:

- Content must be perceivable.
- User interface components in the content must be operable.
- Content and controls must be understandable.
- Content must be robust enough to work with current and future technologies.

WCAG 2.0 does not propose a drastic change from WCAG 1.0. For a comparison of WCAG 1.0 and WCAG 2.0, see www.w3.org/WAI/GL/2005/06/30-mapping.html.

Official guidelines and checkpoints are vital, but they do not cover implementation details for programmer and developer. To help web developers, the W3C provides reference documents with overviews of HTML, CSS, and core techniques at www.w3.org/WAI/intro/wcag.php.

Summary

Several HCI evaluation methods were covered including inspection, lab testing and survey and customer reporting methods. The heuristic evaluation method was covered in detail and the Neilsen's heuristics included for heuristic evaluation analysis. Checklists were covered as a supporting tool for heuristic evaluations and an introduction to automated tools with emphasis in web site interaction evaluation was included with some samples. Finally, web accessibility was defined and the Web Accessibility Initiative covered and main standards introduced.

References

Chandler, K. and Hyatt, K. 2002, *Customer-Centered Design: A New Approach to Web Usability*, Prentince-Hall.

Kalbach, J. 2007, *Designing Web Navigation*, O'Reilly Publications.

Instone, K. 2007, Navigation Stress Test, [Online] Available http://instone.org/navstress/ [Accessed 12 April 2008]

Navarro, A. 2000,. *XHTML by experience*. Que publications.

Nielsen, J. 1994,. Heuristic evaluation. In Nielsen, J., and Mack, R.L. (Eds.), *Usability Inspection Methods*, John Wiley & Sons, New York, NY.

Discussion questions

1. Discuss the pros and cons of using Heuristic Evaluations in interaction design projects.

2. Review the navigation of a local online newspaper in your area. Take notes on the following aspects:
   - Balance: is the site balanced without unnecessary levels?
   - Efficiency: is the navigation efficient to use?
   - Feedback: is it clear where you are in the site?
   - Labeling: are navigation labels clear and understandable?
   - Consistency and inconsistency: is inconsistency used wisely?
   - Visual design: does the visual design of the navigation enhance its use?
   - Appropriateness: is the navigation appropriate for an online newspaper? Does it help you find what you need?

   Pick the one you like best and compare it to the web site for your favorite band or movie. What are the differences?

3. Together with a friend or someone you know, conduct an informal checklist review and a navigation stress test on your favorite e-commerce site. Compare notes and discuss. Where do the findings overlap between a checklist review and the stress text? What differed between the two? Which was more telling about the overall navigation system? (you can use the test stress questions at http://instone.org/navstress and check list at http://www.stcsig.org/usability/topics/articles/he-checklist.html

Activities

For this chapter, you will continue with your interaction design project and will be introduced to Web accessibility testing. You will have to produce two deliverables. First, you will be responsible for the submission of a document that defines the heuristic evaluation activity. Second, you will conduct Web accessibility test and will report your findings.

For the physical prototype produced in chapter 5, produce a heuristic Evaluation. Produce a check list of heuristics that can be used for your design similar to the one at http://www.stcsig.org/usability/topics/articles/he-checklist.html.

Give the list to at least two reviewers that in your opinion might make a good evaluator for the type of interaction you are designing (you could ask your class mates). Please include a report of findings in terms of potential problems and rank them according to Nielsen's rank of severity.

Consider one of the several programs and services that run automated accessibility checks across a web site. These tools crawl through your code and compare it to known standards guidelines and then highlight potential problems. Select one tool from the list below and use it to evaluate any web site of your choice.

- **Wave** (http://wave.webaim.org).
- **A-Checker** (http://checker.atrc.utoronto.ca/)
- Accessibility Check (http://www.etre.com/tools/accessibilitycheck/)

Prepare a report with your findings.

Activities Sample Solution

A) Heuristic Evaluation of Prototype

Report on Heuristic Evaluation - A System Checklist

The following areas of evaluation from the STCSIG example were considered in relation to the nature of the interactions being tested, namely, downloading forms (enrolment, job application) and login (student extranet). Questions were selected from the following three groups:

1. Visibility of System Status

2. Match Between System and the Real World

3. User Control and Freedom

There are some differences in responses from the evaluators. This may have been due to ambiguity relating to what was included as being part of the application. In fact, downloading and printing a document from a website incorporates three interaction interfaces in one computer screen. While one user seems to have considered only the website's navigation and logic, the other user saw the different interactions as a totality, making generalizations about the

1. Website interface,
2. Browser interface and
3. Printer interface.

For instance, returning to a previous page was considered a NO for one tester based on the lack of breadcrumb in the actual HTML pages, but a yes for the other tester because of the ubiquitous back button of the browser and the display (assumed) of meaningful <title> tags content in the drop down box of that button.

| | Evaluator 1 | | | Evaluator 2 | |
Review Checklist	Yes No N/A	Comments	Yes No N/A	Comments
Does every display begin with a title or header that describes screen contents?	N	Job page	Y	
Is there a consistent icon design scheme and stylistic treatment across the system?	Y		Y	
Is a single, selected icon clearly visible when surrounded by unselected icons?	N		N	
Do menu instructions, prompts, and error messages appear in the same place(s) on each menu?	Y		Y	
In multipage data entry screens, is each page labeled to show its relation to others?	Y		Y	
If overtype and insert mode are both available, is there a visible indication of which one the user is in?	N/A		N/A	
If pop-up windows are used to display error messages, do they allow the user to see the field in error?	N/A		N/A	
Is there some form of system feedback for every operator action?	Y		Y	The page changes
After the user completes an action (or group of actions), does the feedback indicate that the next group of actions can be started?	Y		Y	
Is there visual feedback in menus or dialog boxes about which choices are selectable?	Y		Y	
Is there visual feedback in menus or dialog boxes about which choice the cursor is on now?	Y		Y	
If multiple options can be selected in a menu or dialog box, is there visual feedback about which options are already selected?	N/A		N/A	
Is there visual feedback when objects are selected or moved?	Y		Y	
Is the current status of an icon clearly indicated?	Y		N/A	

Is there feedback when function keys are pressed?	Y		Y	
If there are observable delays (greater than fifteen seconds) in the system's response time, is the user kept informed of the system's progress?	N		Y	Loading box at bottom of browser
Are response times appropriate to the task?	Y		Y	
Typing, cursor motion, mouse selection: 50-1 50 milliseconds	Y		Y	
Simple, frequent tasks: less than 1 second	N/A		Y	
Common tasks: 2-4 seconds	N/A		Y	
Complex tasks: 8-12 seconds	N/A		Y	
Are response times appropriate to the user's cognitive processing?	Y		Y	
Continuity of thinking is required and information must be remembered throughout several responses: less than two seconds.	Y		Y	
High levels of concentration aren't necessary and remembering information is not required: two to fifteen seconds.	Y		Y	
Is the menu-naming terminology consistent with the user's task domain?	Y		Y	
Does the system provide *visibility:* that is, by looking, can the user tell the state of the system and the alternatives for action?	Y		Y	
Do GUI menus make obvious which item has been selected?	N		N	
Do GUI menus make obvious whether deselection is possible?	Y		Y	
If users must navigate between multiple screens, does the system use context labels, menu maps, and place markers as navigational aids?	Y		Y	
Are icons concrete and familiar?	N/A		Y	
Are menu choices ordered in the most logical way, given the user, the item names, and the task variables?	Y		N	Reorder top menu

If there is a natural sequence to menu choices, has it been used?	Y		Y	
Do related and interdependent fields appear on the same screen?	Y		Y	
If shape is used as a visual cue, does it match cultural conventions?	Y		Y	
Do the selected colors correspond to common expectations about color codes?	N/A		N/A	
When prompts imply a necessary action, are the words in the message consistent with that action?	Y		Y	
Do keystroke references in prompts match actual key names?	Y		Y	
On data entry screens, are tasks described in terminology familiar to users?	Y		Y	
Are field-level prompts provided for data entry screens?				
For question and answer interfaces, are questions stated in clear, simple language?	Y		Y	
Do menu choices fit logically into categories that have readily understood meanings?	Y		Y	
Are menu titles parallel grammatically?	Y		Y	
Does the command language employ user jargon and avoid computer jargon?	Y		Y	
Are command names specific rather than general?	Y		Y	
Does the command language allow both full names and abbreviations?	N/A		N/A	
Are input data codes meaningful?	Y		Y	
Have uncommon letter sequences been avoided whenever possible?	Y		Y	
Does the system automatically enter leading or trailing spaces to align decimal points?	N/A		N/A	

Does the system automatically enter a dollar sign and decimal for monetary entries?	N/A		N/A	
Does the system automatically enter commas in numeric values greater than 9999?	Y		Y	
Do GUI menus offer activation: that is, make obvious how to say *"now do it"?*	Y		Y	
Has the system been designed so that keys with similar names do not perform opposite (and potentially dangerous) actions?	Y		Y	
Are function keys labeled clearly and distinctively, even if this means breaking consistency rules?	N/A		N/A	

B) Web Accessibility Check of www.polytechnic.bh

Submitting the URL of the home page for a local university produced the following result in WAVE.

"Uh oh! WAVE has detected 28 accessibility errors"

The following are present in the head section or apply to this page in general:

- This page has no headings or document structure so an outline cannot be generated

Most of the errors relate to the lack of text for the ALT attribute of images. This is one of the basic lessons of any introductory web design course and should not have been overlooked by a professional digital agency. The labelling of images is an important way of getting more users, especially those who like to use the images section of Google to find the content they are looking for. This site is image and animation rich which slows down the download time - all the more reason to supply ALT texts.

The 28 errors are repeated instances of the following:

- ALERT: Missing Structure
- "This page has no headings or document structure."
- A table is present that does NOT have any header cells
- ERROR: Linked image missing alt text: Alternative text is not provided for an image that is the sole contents of a link
- ALERT: Problematic link text: Link text does not make sense out of context, contains extraneous text (such as "click here"), or is the same as another link on the page, but links to a different location.
- ERROR: Spacer image missing alt text: Alternative text is not present for an image used as a layout spacer
- ERROR: Form label missing: A form <input>, <select>, or <textarea> does not have a corresponding label. (Note: Labels are not required for hidden, image, submit, reset, or button form elements.)

- ERROR: Image button missing alt text: Alternative text is not present in a form image button
- ERROR: Missing alt text: Alternative text is not present for an image

Chapter 8

Usability testing

In chapter 8, the basics of usability testing are covered. The chapter will cover how to design, prepare and perform usability testing.

Usability testing

After the design on the interaction, it is important to test it by letting users preview it and provide feedback so you can make changes as needed before you release it to the public.

Usability testing answers four key questions about an interaction.
(1)   learnability – how easy does the learning take place?,
(2)   throughput – how easy is it to use?,
(3)   flexibility – how easy is it to change in environment and tasks?,
(4)   attitude – doe it provide the user with a positive attitude?.

Usability testing helps to determine how people use systems and where they may encounter difficulty of use. There is ample evidence that development costs are reduced significantly as a result of employing usability techniques (Sun Microsystems, http://interface.free.fr/Archives/SUN_usability_benefits_Cost.pdf). Training and support costs are also reduced. Landauer (1995) suggests that user-centered approaches reduce training time by 25 percent.

One the main challenges of this type of testing is to define the variables that measure usability. There has been some work that attempted to define variables that can be linked to usability. Eason (1988) defined user independent and user dependent variables that can be linked to the measurement of user interface usability.

Table 1 Usability independent and dependent variables

Independent Variables	Dependent Variables
User Characteristics: Knowledge Discretion Motivation	User reaction-cost benefit analysis (Positive outcome) Good task system match Continued user learning
System Functions: Task match Ease of use Ease of learn	User reaction-cost benefit analysis (Negative outcome) Restricted use Non-use, partial use Distant use
Task Characteristics Frequency Openness	

Eason (1988) mentions that when performing usability evaluations in controlled environments, the study should measure the user reaction. Eason suggests that an individual using a system performs a cost/benefit analysis and achieve either a positive or negative outcome. If it is a negative outcome, the user restricts his or her use of the system possibly to total non use since he or she feels that it costs just too much to use the system compared to the potential benefits. When the outcome is positive, a user judges it beneficial to continue to invest time in further learning of the system.

Shackel (1990) is one of the founding fathers of ergonomics, defined usability measures for user interface design. In Shackel (1990), he proposed that usability could be specified and measured by a set of operational criteria. Terms are assigned numerical values when goals are set during the requirements specification. A summary of his measures are included in table 2.

Table 2 Usability measures

Measure	Comments
Effectiveness	At better than some required level of performance (in terms of speed and errors.)
	By some required percentage of the specified target range of users
	Within some required proportion of the range of usage environments
Learnability	Specified time from installation and start of training
	Based upon some specified amount of training
	Some specified relearning time for intermittent users
Flexibility	Allowing adaptation to some percentage variation in tasks beyond those first specified [difficult to determine in practice and can be replaced by usefulness—achievement of users' goals]
Attitude	Within acceptable levels of human cost in terms of tiredness, discomfort, frustration, and personal effort

There are different lifecycle models for usability testing. However, most of them share the same idea of different phases that are used to design, prepare and perform usability testing. One is the Dumas and Redish (1999) usability testing model that identifies three phases required for usability testing which are:
1. Defining usability testing
2. Conducting the usability test
3. Analyzing and presenting usability test results

Defining Usability testing

Dumas and Redish (1999) identify five tasks that you must complete as you define your usability test:

94

1. Define your goals and concerns.
2. Determine who your test participants are.
3. Select, organize, and create test scenarios.
4. Determine how you will measure usability.
5. Prepare your test materials.

In the first step, goals are identified from different sources (Dumas & Redish 1999):

- Task analysis and quantitative usability goals.
- Timely issues, such as having to produce a usability study to resolve a dispute about whether to add a feature.
- A heuristic evaluation or an expert review, such as concerns from an internal customer (for example, marketing) that need to be addressed.
- Previous tests of this product or other products. One test may provoke concerns that require another test.

In the second step, participants are selected for the usability test. Participants are selected based on characteristics that all users share and those that may cause differences between the users. Following are the decisions you need to make when determining characteristics (Dumas & Redish 1999):

- Users' experience with computers or the product you're testing.
- Users' work experience
- Users' experience with your product
- Users' experience with similar products

In few words, it is important that the test subjects are representative of the real target system but also it is important to include an appropriate number of users to test. Nielsen (2000) argues, based on simple regression to the mean, that five representative users will provide the evaluator with the bulk of usability problems per test over the course of three tests. If the HCI that is being tested has been designed for several distinct user populations, the tester needs to test five users in each of those groups. Nielsen suggests testing fewer users with more tests, during the course of an iterative design, for best results.

Testing every single task is almost impossible so it is important to create test scenarios as indicated in the third step of the usability definition test. Test scenarios should be designed to detect potential usability problems. Test scenarios are normally prepared based on the HCI designer's experiences on what the user will do with the product.

Test scenarios should identity the tasks and hardware and software to perform the tasks. The test case should number each task to complete it and provide and a description for each task that is clear enough for the user to perform it. Because it is not possible to test every possible usage scenario, it is important to prioritize what areas of the HCI need to be usable. The top seven to ten of these tasks should be featured in a usability test. Each task should show the time it will take, the hardware and software needed, and the high-level instructions and procedures required to complete the task. The test scenarios can have the participants stop between each task, such as after a longer task or require distributing a printed questionnaire to all participants after each task.

The fourth step of defining usability tests requires determining usability measures performance and subjective measures. Performance measures are quantitative measures of specific actions and behaviours that are observed during the test while subjective measures are people's perceptions, opinions, and judgments.

Performance measures can be detected by logging each time a user exhibits a certain behaviour during the test, like expressing frustration. Subjective measures are harder to quantify unless more than one participant mentions the same problem such a problem finding a specific button on the screen. Logging usability data can be used with the help of software such as the OVO logger (http:// http://www.ovostudios.com/ovologger_04.asp).

When data is being logged, the test scenario designer might need to define a set criteria for performance measures. A typical criterion for performance measures is a four-point scale, which forces a choice toward positive or negative because there is no strictly neutral response.

The fifth step of defining usability tests requires defining test materials such as testing scripts and legal forms. Before the test is performed, legal forms need to be prepared and should state each party's rights and must ensure that all test participants have read and understand the form. The test should also include a testing script in order to test all users in all groups the same way.

Part of the definition of the test materials is to define the test method to use. There are different types of usability tests. Rubin (1994) identified four types of usability test: exploration, assessment, comparison and validation. Exploration tests are used to make determination about the completeness of a design. Assessment tests are used to investigate physical designs such as paper prototypes and wireframes. Comparison tests are used to explore alternative designs and make determinations about competing solutions and Validation tests are normally used to see how the design works as an integrated solution.

Written questionnaires should be given to test users before the test, after each task, or at the conclusion of test to gather the following information:

- Pretest: This can be used to gather demographic information such as name, gender, and internet experience. An example of this questionnaire can be seen at http://www.utexas.edu/learn/usability/entrance.doc.
- Posttask: This test gathers the opinions and ratings about each task in the test scenario. During the test, it is recommended to have a facilitator that can lead the test subject through a series of questions/tasks. An example of this type of questionnaire can be seen at http://www.utexas.edu/learn/usability/test.doc.
- Posttest: This test has the intention to gather opinions and ratings about the interaction after the test scenario. An example of this type of questionnaire can be seen at http://www.utexas.edu/learn/usability/exit.doc.

Conducting the Usability Test

Before conducting the usability test, it is important to assess the performance of the test by first conducting a pilot test. A pilot test allows to "debug" the test and find out if there are any initial problems with the interaction under test. Problems that can be encountered as issues such as problems performing a task due to bugs with software and hardware, confusing questions, unable to complete tasks and unclear instructions.

Usability tests might be conducted in usability testing laboratories. Testing laboratories are equipped with special observational equipment such as video cameras, hidden observation points, and specially instrumented computers and workstations. If labs are not available another viable solution is to go to the customer's location.

When going to the customer's location, Hackos and Redish, (1998) suggested that the tester should greet the manager and the users, as well as the users' colleagues if they share space and ask for permission to set up your space and the audio and visual equipment, if needed when he or she arrives on site. The tester should make the visit as cooperative as possible and ensure that you build a good relationship with the users, and help them feel reassured when necessary. The test should take notes as an observer, the notes should include information such as the project name, date of the observation, user's goal, user task, notes about user and environment, time the task started, time task stopped, notes that show that the usability goal was met. During the test, the tester should always observe problems and create a problem list.

Users can be interviewed as they are performing the task, but also different types of interviews can be conducted to support your views better as the ones suggested by Hackos and Redish (1998):

- Immediate recall interview— The interviewer should record what the users do, and then talk about what they did at the completion of the task.
- Cued recall interview— The interviewer should record what the users do, and then talk about it sometime later, perhaps with the assistance of video playback.
- Process interview— The interviewer could interview users individually or in groups to understand an entire process or workflow.
- Ethnographic interview— The interviewer can interview one user first as a key informant, and then later interview others and conduct observations with discussion during the observations.
- Cued recall or discourse-based interview with artifact walkthrough— In this type, the interviewer collects artifacts from the user and then construct an interview around the artifacts.
- Critical incident interview— The interviewer interviews users about specific situations when you can't observe them yourself.
- Group interview or focus group— The interviewer interviews users individually or in groups about attitudes, desires, preferences, and so on.
- Usability roundtables— The interviewer interviews users away from their work site.
- Customer partnering— The interviewer works with a group of users over time, with interviews as one of the techniques.

Once test is performed, it is a good idea to follow up in order to obtain usability information over a longer period of time. Dumas and Redish (1999) suggest to follow up by having the users fill out a diary questionnaire form, which contains several questions. The tester sends a new form to the users on a regular basis either on follow-up site visits, by email, by fax, or even by regular mail. The form can have many of the same questions as well as several specific questions so the tester can get answers.

Analyzing and Presenting Usability Test Results

A usability test generates a lot of information that can be analyzed for usability studies. Dumas and Redish (1999) identified that data that should be collected as part of a usability test. The data include the following:

- A list of problems from the test

- Quantitative data on times, errors, and other performance measures, including subjective ratings on questionnaires
- Testers' comments from logs, notes, and questionnaires
- The testing team's written notes
- Background data on the participants
- Videotapes of the test, perhaps from several different viewpoints in the room

The first step in analyzing the data is to tabulate and summarize quantitative data and compile all the comments. Data can be analyzed for trends and descriptive and inferential statistics can be generated for the questionnaires responses and quantitative data. A useful technique for processing data is triangulating it. This involves looking at all the data together to see how each set of data supports the other sets. The data sets are (Dumas and Redish, 1999):

- The problem list
- Quantitative data from logs and questionnaires
- Testers' comments and the testing team's observations

The Data is measured against usability goals and the quantitative criteria that was set before the test to determine what the problems are inside the triangle.

Dumas and Redish (1999) recommend that the analysis should follow some guidelines to make statistical analysis as relevant as possible:

1. Use inferential statistics only if you understand how to apply and interpret them.
2. After you employ a statistical test, carefully explain what the test means.
3. Describe your interpretation of key data values when you don't compute statistical tests. This description will provide your readers with some guidance on the accuracy of "eyeball" tests.

Both your quantitative data analysis as well as the qualitative data from feedback and notes will help you organize the information into two areas (Dumas and Redish, 1999):

- Scope— How widespread is the problem? It's best to organize problems into general groups that indicate a significant problem that's backed up by more specific results from the test.
- Severity— How critical is the problem? You can set up severity criteria as you analyze the data, or you can do so before the test takes place.

A final report should be prepared to summarize the results of the test. Dumas and Redish, (1999) suggest the following sections for a usability test:

- Procedures
- Evaluator profiles
- Observations
- Evaluator quotes
- Conclusions
- Recommendations

A sample usability report and data analysis can be downloaded from the link below:

http://www.utexas.edu/learn/usability/report.html

Summary

This is the end of the book, the book gave you an overview of the different HCI methods and technologies required for the modern information systems professional. During this module, different human computer interaction paradigms were analyzed with the 5W+H heuristic process. Different interaction styles were covered and their benefits and disadvantages were discussed for different interaction applications.

Different techniques to discover requirements were discussed in this module. Conceptual design techniques and interaction models were introduced as useful tools for analyzing and understanding interface design.

In addition, Interface design guidelines were covered and some examples emphasized. The auditory interaction, voice interface model included and haptic technologies were explained and their relevancy to HCI emphasized.

Several HCI methods were covered including inspection, lab testing and survey and customer reporting methods. The heuristic evaluation method was covered in detail.

Usability testing was defined and the different variables that affect usability identified. Usability measures were discussed and the the Dumas and Redish (1999) usability testing model was covered in detail by exploring the defining, conducting and analyzing and presenting results phases.

References

Dumas, J. S., and Redish J.C. 1999 *A Practical Guide to Usability Testing.* Portland, OR, Intellect Books.

Eason, K. 1988. *Information Technology and Organisational Change.* London: Taylor & Francis.

Hackos, J T., and Redish J. C. 1998. *User and Task Analysis for Interface Design.* New York, John Wiley & Sons.

Landauer, Thomas K. 1995, *The Trouble with Computers*, MIT Press, Cambridge, MA.

Rubin, J. 1994, *Handbook of usability testing: How to plan, design, and conduct effective tests.* New York. Wiley.

Shackel, B. 1990. "*Human factors and usability.*" In J. Preece & L. Keller (Eds.) Human-Computer Interaction: Selected Readings. Hemel Hempstead: Prentice-Hall.

Nielsen, J. 2000. Alertbox, why you only need to test with 5 users. [Online]

Available http://www.useit.com/alertbox/200000319.html [Accessed 13 June 2008].

Discussion questions

1. Write a report on an existing usability lab technology. You must include the specifications for the lab's hardware and software. Discuss what kinds of usability testing the particular lab is designed to perform and how the testing can be integrated into any relevant design projects.

2. Discuss how usability differs from utility.

3. Discuss the relationship of usability and effectiveness.

4. Discuss what data should be gathered about a user when performing a usability test.

Activities
For this chapter, you will finalize your interaction design project. You will be responsible for the submission of the full interaction design project that includes all the documents generated in the previous week including the document that defines the usability test activity:

The usability test document should address the following questions:
    Why are you testing?
- Define the Purpose
    What are you testing?
- Define your Concerns and Goals
- Define the Tasks
- Create the Scenarios
- Define the Measurements
    How will you test?
        Define the test method
    Where will you test?
- Determine the location of the tests
    Who will be involved?
- Select Participants, Testers and Observers

    When will you test?
- Create a test schedule
    Writing Scripts:
- Introduction and Instructions
- Testing Interaction
- Debriefing

Activities sample solution

The usability test document
Why are we testing?
Definition of the Purpose
Purpose Statement: the design for interaction on the proposed new website will be tested for possible effects on the number of helpdesk requests the university is currently fielding. The test will provide an idea of user satisfaction levels and an indication of how to modify the design to increase ease and speed of use. The test will also help resolve some of the different points of view among university staff on whether time and money should in fact be devoted to transferring such tasks online: many staff members believe that few users will in fact use the online service, preferring for cultural reasons to have face to face interaction even if this proves more time consuming. There is a widespread belief that trust in online services has not been sufficiently built up in the local culture to warrant the effort and expense and that funds should instead be diverted to improving the comfort of visitors to the campus face-to-face environment.

The website will be viewed through a PC using a standard browser (v4+). Navigation and selection will be performed using a standard mouse and keyboard. Speakers will be necessary to hear some of the animated multimedia presentations contained within some of the pages. Many brochures will be presented for downloading in PDF format: it is assumed that most users will have the option of printing the documentation for reading away from the computer screen.

The different areas of the site will be accessible by;
* A menu based navigation system combining 6 -8 top menu items with submenus of no more than six clickable links that appear in drop down style with the mouseover event.
* A search engine, programmed to perform fuzzy matching with possible misspelled word, and linked to a database of page descriptions

The site will be visited by users in a home or work environment, perhaps in preparation for a visit to the campus, or simply to help in the choice of universities and courses. A version of the site will be compatible with smaller mobile devices (iPad and iPhone). The site will be accessible at any time of day. Visit to the site will probably rise during the two major enrollment periods of the year.

It is expected that the vast majority of visitors will be school leavers, currently enrolled students and the parents or friends of both. The main task set by visitors will concern locating and perhaps printing data that helps them make informed choices about their tertiary studies. These considerations will inform many factors in the test, especially the environment in which the test is conducted, and the choice of users who take the test.

What are we testing?
Definition of our Concerns and Goals
Concerns: The designers are concerned that the users may find the navigation unclear and that they will stray from the quickest path towards their goal of downloading a form or entering a login and password. The three main scenarios will each have a task analysis and an evaluation. With the new enrolment and recruitment season fast approaching, there is a distinct time constraint for rolling out the new "fast track" web navigation.

Goals: That the vast majority of users will respond to the clear interface and recognize on the first attempt the fast track to the download area and/or login. Ideally, the downloading of documents from the web should be initiated within seven seconds of arriving at the website's home page.

Definition of the Tasks
There are three ways in the new proposed design to achieve the desired goals: through the search engine, through the top level navigations, and through the vertical quick links area. The users will be given tasks that do not specify the best way to proceed. For example, one

of the tasks will be formulated as follows: "You wish to enroll in the Business Degree"; or "You wish to find the results of a recent test you sat for."

The tasks will be performed in an onsite computer lab, using a PC, a Firefox web browser and a broadband internet connection.

Create the Scenarios

You are getting a lift to the university in five minutes, but you know that there will be a lot of traffic and a large queue at student registry. You wish to use the website to save time. Try to get as far through the enrollment process as the time frame and the website allow.

Definition of the Measurements

Quantitative Measurements: the amount of time taken for users to complete each task will be recorded and the number of false starts and errors. At least one hundred users need to be tested for the resulting data to yield any significant trends. These users will be drawn from existing students and staff as well as outside visitors. A chance of winning a prize in a competition will be offered as an incentive for giving up their time.

Qualitative Measurements: These will involve fewer users though the testing time will take longer. Users will be asked to "think aloud" as they navigate through the website and make choices. The words will be recorded for later analysis.

How will we test?

Definition of the test method

There will be three different types of testing methods corresponding to different stages in the design and development process.

Diagnostic testing will take place in the early phase and will be based on user reaction to wireframes and mockup screen shots

Comparative tests will be used during the development phase. This will determine whether there are key usability issues between the three navigational methods offered on the website: top menu navigation, quick lings and search engine. There is concern that the search engine will not be sufficiently fine tuned to deal with spelling mistakes and terminology errors.

Validation tests will be conducted using a working prototype of the new website on a password protected server. The cache will be cleared after each user's session to ensure that download times are equal for each user. Users, therefore, have the chance of measuring true reaction speed of web pages. There has been some concern that the enrolment form – an image-laden PDF file of over 1MB might provoke frustration from users. Other concerns relate to the use of heavy graphics and flash animations that the marketing department has chosen without consideration of usability problems.

Where will we test?

The location of the tests

The tests will be held for the most part in a internet-connected computer lab just next to the reception area of student services. The adjacent room will be equipped with monitors that display the image feed from the CCTV cameras installed in the testing area. A kiosk will be hired for the touch screen version. Other tests will involve slow speed connections, computers with small screens, computers in a home environment and computers in a modern office environment where large high resolution screens are the norm.

Who will be involved?

Participants, Testers and Observers

The **participants** will include four current students, four potential students still attending high school, four parents of school leavers or students, four tutors from diverse faculties.

The **testers** will be hired from a local usability testing firm that has experience in website usability testing.

The **observers** will include the design team, representatives from Student Services and Human Resources, the website project manager and the website development team.

The observers will be in the adjacent room watching directly or at a later date by reviewing the taped sessions. The tester will be in the room with the users and the users will be in front of the computer screens.

When will we test?
Test schedule
Project level: Three months for the implementation of a new interface for the entire website.
Test Preparation level: Test preparation should take ten working days. It should be done in March so that testing can coincide with the period that has the maximum number of new visitors to the university. This ensures that the pool of possible participants will be optimized.
Test execution level: 25 minutes (including introduction and reading)
Task execution level: 5 minutes

Writing Scripts:
Introduction and Instructions
- Hello and welcome.
- How are you?
- We are going to ask you to help us test a new feature of our website.
- Could you please take a seat in front of a computer?
- We want to make our website faster and easier to use.
- We would like you to make suggestions on how to improve our website.
- We would like you to perform three different tasks.
- Could you please think aloud? Tell us your reactions to the interface as you go along.
- Please read the task on the cards in front of you and tell us if you understand each task.

Testing Interaction
[See document from previous week below]

Debriefing
- Did you find the instructions clear?
- Was there anything that you considered difficult to find?
- How often do you use the internet/web?
- Have you seen other universities' websites?

Heuristic and Web accessibility testing
Report on Heuristic Evaluation - A System Checklist
The following areas of evaluation from the STCSIG example were considered in relation to the nature of the interactions being tested, namely, downloading forms (enrolment, job application) and login (student extranet). Questions were selected from the following three groups:
1. *Visibility of System Status*
2. *Match Between System and the Real World*
3. *User Control and Freedom*
There are some differences in responses from the evaluators. This may have been due to ambiguity relating to what was included as being part of the application. In fact, downloading and printing a document from a website incorporates three interaction interfaces in one computer screen. While one user seems to have considered only the website's navigation and logic, the other user saw the different interactions as a totality, making generalizations about the
    4. Website interface,
    5. Browser interface and
    6. Printer interface.
For instance, returning to a previous page was considered a NO for one tester based on the lack of breadcrumb in the actual HTML pages, but a yes for the other tester because of the

ubiquitous back button of the browser and the display (assumed) of meaningful <title> tags content in the drop down box of that button.

Review Checklist	Evaluator 1 Yes No N/A	Comments	Evaluator 2 Yes No N/A	Comments
Does every display begin with a title or header that describes screen contents?	N	Job page	Y	
Is there a consistent icon design scheme and stylistic treatment across the system?	Y		Y	
Is a single, selected icon clearly visible when surrounded by unselected icons?	N		N	
Do menu instructions, prompts, and error messages appear in the same place(s) on each menu?	Y		Y	
In multipage data entry screens, is each page labeled to show its relation to others?	Y		Y	
If overtype and insert mode are both available, is there a visible indication of which one the user is in?	N/A		N/A	
If pop-up windows are used to display error messages, do they allow the user to see the field in error?	N/A		N/A	
Is there some form of system feedback for every operator action?	Y		Y	The page changes
After the user completes an action (or group of actions), does the feedback indicate that the next group of actions can be started?	Y		Y	
Is there visual feedback in menus or dialog boxes about which choices are selectable?	Y		Y	
Is there visual feedback in menus or dialog boxes about which choice the cursor is on now?	Y		Y	
If multiple options can be selected in a menu or dialog box, is there visual feedback about which options are already selected?	N/A		N/A	

Is there visual feedback when objects are selected or moved?	Y		Y	
Is the current status of an icon clearly indicated?	Y		N/A	
Is there feedback when function keys are pressed?	Y		Y	
If there are observable delays (greater than fifteen seconds) in the system's response time, is the user kept informed of the system's progress?	N		Y	Loading box at bottom of browser
Are response times appropriate to the task?	Y		Y	
Typing, cursor motion, mouse selection: 50-1 50 milliseconds	Y		Y	
Simple, frequent tasks: less than 1 second	N/A		Y	
Common tasks: 2-4 seconds	N/A		Y	
Complex tasks: 8-12 seconds	N/A		Y	
Are response times appropriate to the user's cognitive processing?	Y		Y	
Continuity of thinking is required and information must be remembered throughout several responses: less than two seconds.	Y		Y	
High levels of concentration aren't necessary and remembering information is not required: two to fifteen seconds.	Y		Y	
Is the menu-naming terminology consistent with the user's task domain?	Y		Y	
Does the system provide visibility: that is, by looking, can the user tell the state of the system and the alternatives for action?	Y		Y	
Do GUI menus make obvious which item has been selected?	N		N	
Do GUI menus make obvious whether deselection is possible?	Y		Y	
If users must navigate between multiple screens, does the system use context labels, menu maps, and place markers as navigational aids?	Y		Y	

Question				
Are icons concrete and familiar?	N/A		Y	
Are menu choices ordered in the most logical way, given the user, the item names, and the task variables?	Y		N	Reorder top menu
If there is a natural sequence to menu choices, has it been used?	Y		Y	
Do related and interdependent fields appear on the same screen?	Y		Y	
If shape is used as a visual cue, does it match cultural conventions?	Y		Y	
Do the selected colors correspond to common expectations about color codes?	N/A		N/A	
When prompts imply a necessary action, are the words in the message consistent with that action?	Y		Y	
Do keystroke references in prompts match actual key names?	Y		Y	
On data entry screens, are tasks described in terminology familiar to users?	Y		Y	
Are field-level prompts provided for data entry screens?				
For question and answer interfaces, are questions stated in clear, simple language?	Y		Y	
Do menu choices fit logically into categories that have readily understood meanings?	Y		Y	
Are menu titles parallel grammatically?	Y		Y	
Does the command language employ user jargon and avoid computer jargon?	Y		Y	
Are command names specific rather than general?	Y		Y	
Does the command language allow both full names and abbreviations?	N/A		N/A	
Are input data codes meaningful?	Y		Y	

Have uncommon letter sequences been avoided whenever possible?	Y		Y	
Does the system automatically enter leading or trailing spaces to align decimal points?	N/A		N/A	
Does the system automatically enter a dollar sign and decimal for monetary entries?	N/A		N/A	
Do GUI menus offer activation: that is, make obvious how to say "now do it"?	Y		Y	
Has the system been designed so that keys with similar names do not perform opposite (and potentially dangerous) actions?	Y		Y	
Are function keys labeled clearly and distinctively, even if this means breaking consistency rules?	N/A		N/A	

Lightning Source UK Ltd.
Milton Keynes UK
UKOW02f1859170914

238754UK00001B/70/P